The Strategic Middle Manager

The Strategic Middle Manager

How to Create and Sustain Competitive Advantage

Steven W. Floyd

Bill Wooldridge

Jossey-Bass Publishers • San Francisco

Substantial discounts on bulk quantities of Jossey-Bass books are available to corporations, professional associations, and other organizations. For details and discount information, contact the special sales department at Jossey-Bass Inc., Publishers (415) 433-1740; Fax (800) 605-2665.

For sales outside the United States, please contact your local Simon & Schuster International Office.

Jossey-Bass Web address: http://www.josseybass.com

 Manufactured in the United States of America on Lyons Falls Pathfinder Tradebook. This paper is acid-free and 100 percent totally chlorine-free.

Library of Congress Cataloging-in-Publication Data

Floyd, Steven W., date.
    The strategic middle manager: how to create and sustain competitive advantage/ Steven W. Floyd, Bill Wooldridge.
      p. cm.
    Includes bibliographical references and index.
    ISBN 0-7879-0208-X
    1. Strategic planning. 2. Middle managers. I. Wooldridge, Bill, date. II. Title.
HD30.28.F58   1996
658.4'012—dc20   95-25970

FIRST EDITION
HB Printing 10 9 8 7 6 5 4 3 2

Contents

Preface

Are middle managers, as some have suggested, no longer needed? Has their function become obsolete in the world of restructuring and downsizing? While many are pessimistic about the future of middle managers, in truth, managerial work has never been more exciting. In fact, we believe that the success of leaner, flatter organizations rests decisively on having managers who can effectively lead from the middle.

To thrive in this environment, however, managers must adopt a radically different orientation toward their work. Externally, they must become adept at spotting the strategic significance of evolving technical and market trends. Internally, they must lead, facilitating and championing innovative strategic initiatives appropriate to an ever-changing context. Our model calls for managers to become *reservoirs* of the organization's capacity to accumulate and deploy critical strategic resources.

The purpose of this book is to reshape the reader's understanding of middle management's role in large, complex organizations. Most conceptions of middle management work focus on operating responsibilities, but these become less relevant in restructured firms emphasizing horizontal processes and knowledge responsibility. We take a fresh look at the changing purpose of middle management, describing its strategic role—and value—in what can only be considered a fundamentally new era of organization and management.

Our motivation came from the sharp contrast between what we have been discovering about the strategic value of middle managers and what most of corporate America appears to believe. In a series of research studies begun in 1989, we explored whether involving middle-level managers in strategic decisions mattered, and if so, how. Not only did it matter, but we found that firms whose middle managers were involved actually had higher levels of innovation and financial performance. The finding that was even more surprising for some of our colleagues, however, was that involvement in the *formulation* of strategy was the key to improved performance. That is, when middle managers were involved in the *substance* of strategic decisions—not just in their implementation—the bottom line improved significantly.

In contrast, conventional wisdom paints middle management as a necessary evil at best, and at worst, as excess baggage to be jettisoned in the process of downsizing. There is growing evidence that this view is too narrow and that the widespread elimination of middle managers may be taking its toll. A recent study by the American Management Association concluded that profits rose at only 51 percent of the companies that downsized between 1989 and 1994, productivity improved at only 34 percent of the firms, and morale fell in an overwhelming 86 percent of the organizations.[1] One reason for these results is that indiscriminate, across-the-board cutbacks leave companies without the capabilities they need to compete. As one top manager told us, "There's nobody left around here who knows how to get anything done!"

Thus we felt it was important to share what we have learned about the strategic value of middle managers. For senior executives, the book offers a framework for harnessing the strategic potential of middle managers, thereby increasing the firm's ability to learn, innovate, and develop competitive advantage. The message is also directed squarely at middle managers themselves. Their potential was evident in our statistical samples, but less than 10 percent of the middle managers we studied were living up to their strategic roles.

Managing in a New Context

The pent-up demand and limited competition prevalent from the end of World War II through the 1960s has been displaced by what is being called the era of hypercompetition.[2] To succeed in this environment, firms must continually search for new ways to improve and tailor their products to an increasingly sophisticated and well-served customer base.

In terms of organizational structure there is an emerging consensus about the type of change required. Increasingly, competitive advantage is seen to come more from innovation and customer responsiveness than from volume-driven strategies that use economies of scale and experience effects. Recognizing this, firms are restructuring themselves away from the efficiency-oriented, vertical hierarchies of the past. They are replacing layers of management with horizontally arranged units defined by business processes.

But although there is significant agreement about the design of organizations, there has been much less appreciation for how these new forms affect the jobs of individual managers. A generation ago, most middle managers held formal, line authority over specific functions. They were perhaps best described as "watchdogs" who kept operations on track. Their focus was mainly internal, and they were concerned chiefly with monitoring activities against a predetermined plan.

In today's world, however, even identifying who is a middle manager can be problematic and requires more than a cursory look at job titles. Contemporary middle managers often occupy positions in teams or in horizontal process centers. Their influence comes not from hierarchical authority but instead from a unique knowledge base and an ability to integrate strategic and operating-level information. In this new context, *any individual who is regularly involved in, or interfaces with, the organization's operations and who has some access to upper management has the potential to be a strategic middle manager.*

In essence then, this book is about leading from the middle: moving the organization through a learning process whose goal is the effective accumulation and deployment of organizational capabilities. Our belief is that middle managers are essential to the organization's long-term strategic effectiveness and innovative capacity. Thus, although their numbers may be declining, the strategic importance and influence of middle managers will increase dramatically as firms continue to look for new ways to compete and to become more responsive and adaptable.

Audience

This book is written for three related audiences: middle managers, top managers, and those who may be aspiring to such positions. Our intent in differentiating between top and middle manager audiences is not to pit one against the other or to assess blame. Quite the contrary: clearer expectations for middle management should promote closer ties between the two groups. The book helps top managers see the strategic value of middle managers and shows middle managers what the new expectations are. We hope therefore to strengthen the relationship and reinforce its cooperative foundation, reversing the effects of fear and mistrust accumulated in the downsizing era.

Middle Managers

For middle managers, understanding how to add strategic value is the key to job security. The book identifies what specific activities, knowledge, and skills are cultivated by managers who play strategic roles. Middle managers need to get ahead of the restructuring wave, moving away from the operating and control functions that are made obsolete by new technologies and market changes. In the book's early chapters we introduce the concept of core capability as the basis for competitive advantage and show how middle managers are crucial in both the accumulation and deployment of capability. Chapter Four describes strategy making in behavioral terms, showing how specific middle management activities fit into the picture. Chapters Five through Eight describe each of four key strategic roles. We illustrate both successes and failures so that managers can begin to differentiate effective pursuit of strategic influence from political self-interest.

The strategic roles we describe provide the basis for proactive adjustment, so that middle management readers can be appreciated as sources of capability and competitive advantage. Based on our research, we developed a self-test of managerial strategic value (Resource B). We recommend that middle management readers take the test now—before reading the rest of the book—to get a realistic appraisal of their own behavior.

Top Managers

This book provides top managers a new basis for relating to and utilizing middle management resources, and a new vocabulary to define what they want from middle managers. The description in

Chapter Two of how middle managers create and develop core capability, and the four strategic roles detailed in Chapters Five through Eight will help executives crystallize what is needed most from middle management. Chapter Four describes a process for making strategy that incorporates a new model of middle management involvement and thereby sets the stage for eliciting new expectations. Chapter Nine provides an important extension of existing guidelines about restructuring that make it possible to transform a company without destroying it. This book will help top managers develop a process that sorts out needed organizational muscle from excess managerial fat and that takes advantage of middle management's knowledge and skills.

Aspiring New Professionals

For the thousands just entering the workplace, currently attending business school, or now occupying nonmanagerial positions, the book offers a description of middle management effectiveness that is unavailable elsewhere. It is unfortunately true that most middle-level managers do a poor job of articulating their potential contribution. In sharp contrast to the concrete realities of day-to-day command-and-control, the ability to nurture the development of new capabilities, for example, is difficult to recognize in oneself or in others.

There are plenty of books about the "new management," and many of these are excellent resources. What we have found, however, is that they describe operating roles or management *in general*. Others are not specific about what managers are actually doing and choose instead to characterize the new organizational priorities, structures, and systems. Those that do describe managerial behavior do so without differentiating middle-level from top- and operating-level activity.

This book, however, is quite specific: it describes the activities middle managers can perform to create and sustain competitive advantage. Beyond this, Chapter Ten describes the skills and knowledge base individuals need in order to have a strategic influence. Lifetime employment is a thing of the past, but performance in the strategic roles offers managers a way to secure the future by making themselves essential.

Overview of the Contents

Part One examines changes in the business context in order to explain the need for a new vision of middle management. Chapter One gives a brief history of middle management's rise in corporate America and shows how today's perceptions of middle managers developed from the post–World War II experience. A central point is that most of our assumptions about middle managers no longer apply in the 1990s. Chapter Two chronicles the changing assumptions about the basis of competition. In the new economy, sustained competitive advantage is seen to result more from a firm's ability to develop new capabilities and to learn to do new things than from its attempts to defend established market positions. The strategic importance of learning means that organizations need to be more adaptive, more adept at harmonizing official strategy with conditions at the operating level. This puts a premium on the unique position of middle managers and creates the potential for them to contribute to capability-based advantage.

Chapter Three shows how restructuring efforts have overlooked the changes in management and competition that are described in the first two chapters. The cumulative results of this oversight can be linked to the growing body of evidence concerning restructuring's mixed effects. When premised on obsolete models of management and competition, restructuring *arbitrarily* targets middle managers and thereby risks "throwing the baby out with the bathwater."

By providing this background we risk losing the reader anxious for "hands on" guidance. It is not possible, however, to fully appreciate middle management's role in today's organizations without understanding both how current circumstances came about and the changes now occurring. Still, some readers may grow impatient and prefer to go directly to Part Two, where we detail the specific behaviors that make middle managers strategically indispensable.

Chapter Four looks at the process of making strategy from the perspective of the organization's middle levels and introduces four strategic roles. Each role is unique to middle management and vital to a firm's ongoing effectiveness. Although each role is considered separately, in reality they are intimately interconnected. The chapter ends with an integrative model connecting the four roles and linking the roles to the organization's overall strategy.

Chapters Five through Eight analyze the elements of the four strategic roles. In each case, the discussions thoroughly illustrate and elaborate what we have identified as four new dimensions of management.

Part Three tells managers how to begin unleashing the potential dynamos in the middle of their organizations. Chapter Nine describes the role of executive leadership in harnessing that potential. It also shows how to open up strategic decisions—especially restructuring decisions—to middle management influence. Middle managers have the information needed to make restructuring work, but because they can be seen as prime targets, their involvement has been problematic, to say the least. Chapter 10 offers middle managers a guide for stepping up to the challenge. The focus is on the company-specific knowledge and generic skills needed to perform the strategic roles.

Storrs, Connecticut   Steven W. Floyd
Amherst, Massachusetts   Bill Wooldridge
January 1996

To our wives Beverly and Linda

The Authors

Steven W. Floyd is associate professor of strategic management at the University of Connecticut and a partner in the Strategic Alliance Group, a Massachusetts-based consulting firm. He has held management positions in both the public and private sector, and prior to entering academe he was president of a medium-size manufacturing firm. He received his Ph.D. degree in business administration (1986) from the University of Colorado. His dissertation was funded by a grant from IBM and analyzed the degree of alignment between managerial work and desktop computer usage. He has published work on the managerial implications of information technology in such journals as *Technology Analysis and Strategic Management* and the *Journal of Management Information Systems*. Over the last several years, his research with Bill Wooldridge has focused on strategic decision-making processes. Studies of how strategic consensus influences organizational performance have been published in leading international journals, including the *Strategic Management Journal* and the *Academy of Management Executive*. Since 1990, the research has focused on the strategic contributions of middle managers. Findings on this topic have been published in top scientific journals and featured in the business press.

Professor Floyd has consulted for dozens of organizations to improve the level of understanding and commitment toward strategy. He and Bill Wooldridge offer seminars for middle managers in the new strategic roles. Often tailored for a specific company, the course uses workbooks, exercises, and interactive videos. Dr. Floyd's consulting also includes a specialization in the health care industry, where he facilitates decision-making groups and provides seminars for physicians, hospitals, and other managed care organizations.

Bill Wooldridge is associate professor of strategic management at the University of Massachusetts. He earned his B.S. degree (1976) from Ithaca College and M.B.A. and Ph.D. degrees from the University of Colorado. Before entering academe, Professor Wooldridge held various managerial positions with both manufacturing and service organizations. He has conducted research in and published articles on succession in family enterprise, the strategic implications of information technology, and middle management consensus and involvement in strategy. In 1992 he received the Family Firm Institute's Outstanding Contribution to Research award.

As a facilitator, Professor Wooldridge has helped numerous groups reach consensus about the strategic issues facing their organizations. His seminars with Steven Floyd have received accolades for their effectiveness in creating a new understanding among top and middle-level managers. Professor Wooldridge also emphasizes the power of involvement in his consulting to firms pursuing ISO 9000 certification.

The Strategic Middle Manager

Part One

The New Middle Management Imperative

Chapter One

Leadership from the Middle

The Changing Demands of Middle Management Work

The unprecedented growth of large industrial corporations during the first half of the twentieth century set the stage for the rise of middle management. From 1945 through the 1950s, thousands of working-class veterans, educated by the GI bill, became middle managers in American corporations and created the largest professional middle class of any society in history.

In the 1990s, serious questions are being raised about the future of this broad middle class. Thousands of middle management jobs have been eliminated through corporate restructuring and downsizing. Have middle managers become the dinosaurs of the industrial world? In this chapter we begin to tell the story of middle management's recent past and current circumstances. As the story unfolds, it becomes clear that what today's economy needs is not the elimination of middle management but rather a new vision of leadership from the middle.

Management in the Middle

Although the layman tends to visualize a manager either as a first-level supervisor or as an occupant of the executive suite, the truth is that the vast majority of managers in today's large organizations are middle managers. Their positions are located somewhere between the strategic apex and the operating core of the organization. Traditionally, they have been charged with overseeing some aspect of the organization's operations—what organization theorists would call "subunit work flow"—with one or more layers of management reporting to them. They have had at least some access to upper management. Their responsibilities have been defined mainly according to functional boundaries, and they have held formal authority over operating-level managers, supervisors, and individual contributors.

In "flattened" organizations as well, where functional boundaries are de-emphasized and the number of layers reduced, there are individuals who are middle managers, although this may not be immediately apparent. Often they have no formal line authority or managerial title. They do, however, perform managerial functions, both those traditionally associated with middle managers and, in some firms, those associated with the strategic roles. Identifying who is and who is not a middle manager comes not so much from job titles or formal job descriptions but from how an individual views and approaches his or her responsibilities.

Wherever they are located in the organization, middle managers' distinguishing function is to align the organization's goals and strategies with its operating-level activity. Until fairly recently, this has meant monitoring and controlling organizational behavior against a predetermined set of plans. A short history of how this job has evolved will be useful in understanding why it must change.

The Changing Managerial Context

The steady growth following World War II represented "spoils" of victory that were shared almost exclusively among American businesses. The global marketplace had yet to emerge; Japanese and European industries were busy rebuilding from the war's devastation. For their part, American firms competed only marginally with one another, as the country's demand for consumer goods appeared insatiable.

To meet this demand, the focus of industry centered on efficiency and large-scale manufacturing. Technology at the time was rigid, because long set-up times and retooling costs discouraged anything more than the most modest product innovations. Immense manufacturing facilities, organized by middle managers under the principles of scientific management, churned out millions of automobiles, appliances, and televisions.

Managing these operations was largely an exercise in administration. Demand was steadily growing and could be realistically forecast. Model changes were rare and could be introduced according to a planned cycle. The trick, then, was simply to keep the "machine" running, and thousands of middle managers were hired as overseers and problem solvers. Middle management itself became a growth industry, and by the early 1960s white-collar positions had overtaken blue-collar jobs as a source of employment in the U.S. manufacturing sector.[1]

Because strategy was fairly stable in most companies, middle managers of the time could be described as "watchdogs" who kept things on track. Their focus was internal: they were chiefly concerned with planning for growth, monitoring costs, identifying variances, and resolving problems that operating managers could not handle. In brief, middle managers during this period oversaw the execution of a calculated, formal strategy that was articulated explicitly in detailed plans. While the activities of middle management in the post-war era were appropriate at the time, their legacy continues as a source of confusion about middle management in today's business context.

Management as a Profession

The growth in middle management employment in the U.S. economy fueled institutional tendencies toward "professionalizing" the occupation. Programs in business administration and management emerged on college campuses across the country, and the American Management Association was created to advance the practice of management. The M.B.A. did not confer the social status of an M.D. or J.D., but it frequently could confer the salary. Equally important, credentialing set middle managers apart from other members of the organization. They were more than just white-collar workers or supervisors. They were the epitome of corporate commitment, and the core of corporate strength.

By the 1960s, textbooks had firmly established the role of middle management in large organizations. Even today, the sequential "plan, organize, direct, and control" model of management is often taught in U.S. business schools. Top management, it is said, creates plans and organizational arrangements, while middle management directs and controls operations. Thus, the perceptions of even the youngest managers have been shaped by the experience of the past.

Shifting Managerial Priorities

In today's economy, global competitors, demanding customers, and rapidly changing technologies have caused firms to shift their priorities from growth and control to innovation and customer responsiveness. As the pace of change has increased, the importance of planning, monitoring, and controlling activity has decreased. Middle managers are increasingly being called upon to focus on the "what" of strategy, sharpening top management's vision by developing and promoting initiatives that respond to changing conditions.

In far too many organizations, however, the needed shift in middle management's orientation has not occurred. While much has been written about the new environment, expectations for middle management have become amorphous. An ample vocabulary has developed to articulate what is *not* needed (for example, layers of administration), but for the most part, sources are mute on what *is* required from those in the middle. This ambivalence toward middle management is perhaps best illustrated by the fact that General Electric and other companies are avoiding use of the term "middle manager" altogether, renaming these positions with titles such as "business leader." The title points to new expectations and a complete reorientation of middle management work.

Dimensions of a Reorientation in Middle Management

Table 1.1 summarizes the important differences between the managerial context in the post-war era and today. Although each of these shifts has been discussed elsewhere, the point here is that they set a whole new stage for managerial action. Notice, too, that each shift tends to move organizations and the role of middle management in a similar direction: toward a world of work where everything is in flux and where learning is the only stable goal. Taken as a whole, these developments require a fundamental reorientation in middle management work, the dimensions of which are identified in Table 1.2.

Table 1.1. The Changing Historical Context of Middle Management Work.

Variable	Post-War Era	Today
Employment growth	Agriculture to manufacturing	Manufacturing to service and knowledge work
Economic demand	Pent-up and growing	Level and declining
Customers	Pliant with similar preferences	Demanding with varied preferences
Competition	Friendly and domestic	Intense and global
Technology	Incremental change	Continuous dramatic change

Table 1.2. The Changing Orientation of Middle Management Work.

Traditional Orientation of Tasks	Contemporary Orientation of Tasks
Developing coordination within functional boundaries	Achieving relationships across organizational boundaries (Boundary-spanning)
Controlling growth	Finding innovation (Championing initiatives)
Executing plans	Encouraging an evolving mindset (Synthesizing information)
Applying new technologies to production	Transferring technology within the organization (Facilitating learning)

From Coordinating Within the Corporation to Managing Relationships Across Organization Boundaries

More and more managers work in service- and knowledge-based organizations. This is due not only to the natural growth in these sectors but also to organizational trends taking place throughout the economy. As part of restructuring, many large firms have begun to outsource less central tasks that were formerly done in-house. As a result, a new breed of smaller firms offering specialized business services has begun to develop.

Another by-product of restructuring has been the emulation of supplier/customer relationships within the organization. Process centers and work teams increasingly are charged with serving "internal customers." Thus, even within manufacturing environments, more and more of the activities of business are service based.

Service organizations are more relationship oriented for two reasons. First, the clients they encounter tend to have more varied problems, as compared to the customer looking for a particular product. At the extreme, services may be customized to meet the special needs of each buyer. Assessing customer requirements, designing solutions, and delivering services thus require intensive interface between the service provider and customer. Second, services are frequently delivered through an integrated network of independent firms or strategic alliances. In these settings, building and maintaining productive relationships becomes a central managerial focus.

Relationship-oriented middle management is ubiquitous in the rapidly growing health care industry, for example. A typical regional manager for a large health maintenance organization (HMO) relies on a variety of relationships: with employers to sell the firm's service; with physicians to provide care; with hospitals, clinics, pharmacies, and labs to provide support; and with members to maintain market share. Thus HMOs are populated by middle managers with such titles as manager of provider relations, manager of member relations, manager of hospital relations, and so on. These positions are charged not only with coordinating the "seamless" delivery of care but also with orchestrating innovation and facilitating change in a highly competitive environment.

So, as the work becomes more service based, today's middle manager is more likely focused on the management of external relationships and the development of novel arrangements among internal partners. Rather than operating within a business function, the new, *boundary-spanning* middle manager promotes integration, coordination, and innovation across borders both within and between organizations.

From Controlling Growth to Finding Innovation

Changes in consumer demand and more intense competition have also shifted the priorities of business and have thus changed the job of middle management. With an economy marked by little aggregate savings and with competition offering more and more choices, consumer spending is highly cyclical, and shoppers have become increasingly discriminating. In manufacturing, this has driven a dramatic reduction in cycle times for new products, down to two or three years in automobiles, for instance. In the service and knowledge sectors, the pace of product proliferation is mind-boggling.

Returning to health care, there are literally dozens of ways to organize an HMO, representing an almost infinite variety of arrangements between employers, insurers, physicians, hospitals, and members. Each of these goes by a different acronym (PHO, PPO, POS, MSO, and so on) and has different implications for the trade-off in patient choice and price. Competition has forced the large HMOs to offer a menu of five, six, or more alternative medical care delivery systems. Patients, who once chose an insurance arrangement for life, have become increasingly fickle, straying from one arrangement to the next as needs change and prices shift. Further, there is continuous pressure to change the mix of services and to innovate, as new rivals enter the market or as new ways to manage care are uncovered.

Business has found that it is no longer enough to offer a line of standard products or services at two or three different price points. As markets become increasingly segmented, being competitive means offering a whole range of specialized outputs with the best features, at the best price. But that's not the end of the story. Producing a successful product invites imitation and enhancement from competitors. Proprietary features quickly become widely available on competing brands. In the service sector, quick imitation of a competitor's approach is frequently required just to survive. Witness the waves of service changes that ebb and flow across the telecommunications and airlines industries. Thus, the strategic middle manager becomes the champion of innovation, finding viable strategic alternatives and gaining acceptance for them within the organization.

From Executing Plans to Encouraging an Evolving Mindset

With the shift from control to innovation, it is not surprising that the relevance of formal planning has also changed. The ability to plan relies on forecasting demand, predicting margins, and establishing long-term objectives, and this ability decreases markedly with decline in the length and stability of product life cycles. Yet, without any form of direction, an innovative organization risks confusion, inconsistent priorities, and economic failure.

Some managers have begun to recognize that consistency and coherence can emerge when a level of strategic understanding is shared among organization members. The mechanisms to achieve this vary widely. One large insurance firm, struggling to increase innovation, has adopted the use of a one-page "strategic agenda" to articulate the company's annual priorities. Together with a long-term vision, the agenda provides an easily comprehensible framework within which middle managers can focus their attention and expand the organization's knowledge base. This process, in turn, advances the learning needed to foster innovative initiatives. Middle management's role in this regard is enhanced by the fact that they are positioned uniquely at the center of the organization's internal social network and at the interface between the organization and its external environment. Strategically aware middle managers therefore play a key part, interpreting information and influencing the organizational mindset.

From Applying New Technologies to Transferring Technology Within the Organization

The final dimension of the reorientation we are suggesting hinges on how managers approach technology. In the past, technology was restricted mostly to the production floor. Today, complex, interactive technology permeates every facet of U.S. industry and seems often to spell the difference between a firm's success or failure. Rather than being used to manage large-scale production, however, new technologies such as computer-aided design/computer-aided manufacturing (CAD/CAM), electronic data interchange (EDI), and e-mail are aimed at helping firms to become more flexible, responsive, and innovative.

Taking advantage of these technologies, however, often rests more on interpersonal and leadership skills than on technical competence. For example, when product concepts developed in R&D are transferred to engineering and manufacturing, functionally oriented personnel in these areas are likely to resent "outsiders" telling them "how to do their jobs." It is up to middle managers to bridge the cross-functional gap and find a way to define the common priorities. Complicating matters is the diversity of personalities and professional orientations within technical organizations. The potential for interpersonal conflict is great, and middle managers who take the lead in cross-functional teams must have an ability to gain cooperation among a group of individuals who rarely see eye to eye. Such conflict resolution is usually accomplished informally, by establishing a working environment where people trust one another. This is no small feat in the face of the resource scarcities and downsizing that are the norm in most organizations.

Thus, a central concern has become how to *facilitate* organizational learning. Managing learning means encouraging information sharing and sheltering experimental behavior. It calls for a set of skills that are often regarded as "soft," "touchy-feely," and even "mushy."

Summary

The realities of today's business environment require a reorientation in middle management work toward managing relationships, finding innovation, creating a mindset, and facilitating learning. In part, the vision for the needed shift evolves from the actions of each manager as he or she faces new challenges and finds ways to cope. But vision is also proactive. It requires reframing one's reality along the dimensions suggested in Table 1.2, and it involves actively searching for solutions and new resources. In Chapter Two, we continue the reframing process by describing the shift in how firms create competitive advantage.

Competing on Capabilities

The Middle Manager's Role in Leveraging Knowledge and Skills

To better understand middle management's role in today's business setting one needs to appreciate how the turbulence characterizing today's economy has affected competitive relationships. Models of competition used to be based on the assumption that firms compete in markets with an established set of competitors. The emphasis was on identifying profitable niches and positioning the firm in ways that avoided head-to-head competition.

Increasingly, however, new technologies are making industry boundaries and stable patterns of competition irrelevant. Almost overnight, it seems, new industries are being created for products not envisioned a short time ago. It is becoming impossible to predict how advancing technologies will affect competition, and more fundamentally, to predict which industries will be affected. Consider the looming possibilities created by the Internet. Retailing, publishing, entertainment, and a host of other markets stand to be turned upside down.

Driving this new, dynamic form of competitive rivalry are global firms not content with small niches in established industries. Gary Hamel and C. K. Prahalad describe, for example, the case of Komatsu, a Japanese upstart in the earth mover industry who defined its "strategic intent" in 1980 as the desire to unseat Caterpillar, the industry leader.[1] Step by step, Komatsu committed its limited resources to the pursuit of a series of ambitious targets that focused squarely on Caterpillar's advantage. The Japanese firm ignored the size of its opposition and its own lack of market power, choosing to compete head-on rather than occupy a niche.

Competing on Capability

Though Caterpillar has since recovered from its battle with Komatsu, the company learned a powerful lesson. To sustain a competitive advantage, firms cannot take their position for granted. Rather, they must continuously redefine their strategies and invest in organizational capabilities that will make them successful.

Returning to the Internet example, there is no doubt that this technology holds ominous possibilities for retailing. Some have suggested that retail outlets in the recorded music business will have reduced significance as consumers increasingly will be able to purchase music directly off the network. The extent to which this occurs and its effect on individual retailers depends on the ability to exploit the opportunity, whether it comes from capabilities developed by those already established in the industry or from the entrepreneurial ability of new entrants.

Increasingly then, competitive advantage is seen to result from the accumulation and deployment of appropriate organizational capabilities. According to this view, the most important ingredients of these capabilities are the knowledge and skills accumulated collectively over time inside an organization. Combined with physical assets like technology and capital, the knowledge and skills of people provide the organization with the capabilities that allow it to compete. When they effectively differentiate a firm from its competitors and thereby create competitive advantage, these capabilities are called *core capabilities*.

Core capabilities are embedded deeply within a firm's sociology, not in specific technologies or in the minds of individuals but in the collective efforts emerging day-to-day from interactions among people over time. Wal-Mart, for example, has developed a set of capabilities focused on its relationships with suppliers. Combined with its unique warehousing system, these relationships convey a significant competitive advantage. This core capability developed initially from Sam Walton's personal ability to negotiate a good deal and from the value he placed on getting the most from suppliers. As the company grew, managers in the firm learned from Sam and at the same time built systems and knowledge of their own that leveraged and amplified the original talent. Today, the organization's core capability is a complex social mix of knowledge, computer-based technology, management systems, and organizational values.

Sustaining Capability-Based Advantage

The historical and socially complex nature of core capability is important. Unlike specific products or technologies that can be copied, core capabilities cannot be reverse-engineered or purchased on an open market. Moreover, intangible assets such as firm reputation tend to attach themselves to capabilities, so that even when a competitor matches the capability on an objective basis, the original firm's image and reputation tends to enhance the durability of its advantage. Because core capabilities and intangible assets are acquired over an extended period in a unique social context, they are difficult, costly, or even impossible to imitate. In a recent survey of chief executives, for example, most said it would take more than ten years "to replace the firm's reputation if it were suddenly lost."[2]

The downside, of course, is that because core capabilities take so long to develop, managers facing challenges from competitors with *new* capabilities may find themselves unable to respond in a timely fashion. Finding oneself without a capability needed to execute a strategy is like running an airline without good ground support.

In fact, the experience of major airline carriers trying to imitate their smaller rivals is instructive. United Airlines and other major carriers have seen their market share in the western United States gobbled up by upstart Southwest Airlines. Southwest is able to fly short, direct flights between major cities at a cost somewhere between 10 and 20 percent below that of the major carriers. No matter how much they try, no one has successfully emulated Southwest's capability. Asked how they do it, Southwest's chief executive attributes his company's success to the people.

Strategy, then, is about acquiring and learning new capabilities. Recently, for example, United announced the creation of a new division configured—like Southwest—exclusively with Boeing

737s and charged with flying direct flights in short hauls along the West Coast. The learning and change that United is going through and their level of success developing these new capabilities represents their *dynamic capability*.

In the end, dynamic capability—the ability to develop new capabilities—is the ultimate source of competitive advantage. Since all core capabilities are likely to become obsolete in the face of new competition, managers face the twin challenge of continuously refining and reinvesting in their existing capabilities while at the same time learning how to do new things. In principle, therefore, dynamic capability is the feature of organizations most likely to be associated with long-term economic performance.

Middle Managers as Reservoirs of Capability

Despite its importance, there has been little research on the managerial behaviors associated with dynamic capability. In one of our own studies of middle managers, however, we discovered a striking correspondence between the nature of organization capability and how middle managers influence the quality of strategy. The connection is no coincidence. Middle managers' role in capability development arises because they are at the nexus of the social interactions that build organizational knowledge and skills.

Think for a moment about an organization as an information network. Information flows between people, so that an individual organization member might be visualized as a point on a web of communication that criss-crosses the organization. Certain points on the organizational web naturally emerge as nodes—places where information of various kinds (for example, technological, market, and financial) comes together in order to direct or coordinate activities.

Top managers represent one sort of node, where a complicated array of internal and external information flows and where, as a result, the knowledge needed to provide overall strategic direction accumulates. Middle managers represent another sort of node, where information flows are typically densest.[3] Here, contacts both inside and outside the organization are more frequent and require more fine-grained detail. There are nodes at the operating level, too, of course, each responsible for producing a particular part of the overall activity. The nodes in the middle, however, are unique because they blend both internal and external information that is related to action as well as direction. It is this feature that makes the knowledge accumulated at middle management levels strategic.

Developing New Capabilities

One of the companies we studied is the baked goods unit of a large, diversified foods producer. But this is no ordinary bakery. Among other things, the company bakes and distributes a line of gourmet cookies and has established an unprecedented, national reputation as the answer for late-night "munchies." Cookies are sold in packages of eight or ten at prices equal to what competitors are only able to charge for dozens. About five years ago, however, the firm began to feel the competitive pinch from a host of smaller bakeries who were selling fresh, gourmet cookies in single servings through convenience stores. These outlets had been an especially lucrative distribution channel, but packaging and distributing the product in quantities of one or two posed a major problem. Existing packages were filled by hand, and the firm was already coping with complaints by employees of carpel-tunnel syndrome, a chronic disease from overuse of the hand. Smaller packages seemed unimaginable.

Fortunately, in response to employee complaints, a production manager in one of the bakeries had been investigating automated packaging systems. He had begun working with an equipment supplier without any explicit direction from above and had even contracted for a mock-up of the new, customized assembly process. His interest and expertise spread to other members of the production team.

When word surfaced that top management wanted to study automated assembly, his plant quickly was identified as the place to start. In six months the pilot project was up and running, and managers from other plants were brought in to learn about the new approach to packaging. Within less than a year, the company had a sophisticated, video-activated robotic packaging line in two of its plants.

Not only had the source and design for the technology been developed, but management and employees in the pilot plant had already begun to build the necessary competencies and willingness to change. This created a knowledge base and a level of social acceptance that significantly quickened the pace at which the firm was able to respond and change.

The middle-level production manager who began thinking about automation did so because he was first to appreciate the significance of the capability barrier facing the company. The stress injuries had taught him that smaller packages were impossible, and he understood the industry well enough to know that the firm would eventually be forced to respond to the competition.

More generally, middle managers' exposure to daily operating problems, such as customer and employee complaints, negotiations with suppliers, tactical moves by competitors, and so on, causes them to be aware of important technical or marketing trends before such issues surface at the top. From the other direction, middle managers are usually responsible for translating top management's goals into action. These implementation responsibilities make middle managers aware of current thinking in the executive suite and provide them with a degree of strategic understanding not prevalent at operating levels.

In short, by virtue of their exposure to both top and operating levels, middle managers gain unique insight into what the organization is able to do and what new capabilities need to be developed. They are crucial "linchpins"—between the firm and its environment and between strategic and operational decision making. This linking function is central in deploying and gaining leverage from existing capabilities and in accumulating new ways of doing things.

Discovering the Limits of Existing Capability

In 1990, the consulting firm Booz-Allen Hamilton published a monograph that identified "making strategy happen" as the critical challenge in the coming decade.[4] Too often, American firms have identified the right strategy but floundered in the followthrough. One of the main reasons for this gap is that top management's plans are often out of sync with organizational realities.

The division president of a large insurance firm, for example, recently planned to make a promise to each of his industrial accounts. The promise was: "An annual safety inspection goes with every insurance contract." This was consistent with loss prevention expertise as the company's competitive advantage. The promise of annual inspections was a good way to gain marketing leverage and premium prices.

As they discovered once middle managers got involved, however, the company had far too few inspectors to fulfill this promise. Moreover, mid-level account managers knew that such a program had limited value to smaller accounts. The company responded by revising the new strategy to incorporate only the largest "Tier 1" accounts.

The lesson here is that one cannot leverage a capability that does not exist, and frequently, middle managers are the only people in a position to know the subtle detail about the depth or breadth of capability within the firm.

Synthesizing the Organizational Knowledge Base

The two examples above illustrate how *individual* managerial knowledge is employed in the development of new capabilities and in recognizing the limits of present capability. At this level, an individual middle manager's knowledge becomes central in an organization's ability to make relatively incremental changes in strategy.

At a deeper level, however, it is important to appreciate how middle managers contribute to the creation of an *organizational* knowledge base. The leap from individual accumulation of knowledge to organizational learning has only recently become a subject of formal investigation, and there is much that remains unknown. Two things appear certain, however. First, some firms perform better than others in their ability to absorb and transfer knowledge within their organizations, and second, this ability is a precursor to technological innovation and radical strategic change.

Again, United States and Japanese competition provides an example. In 1956, Ampex Corporation of Redwood City, California, demonstrated a video tape recorder (VTR) for the first time. Even in those early days, top executives in both Japanese and U.S. television firms realized the huge market potential for home-based systems. Indeed, as early as 1951, David Sarnoff, chairman of RCA, had envisioned a commercially viable VTR. In addition to RCA and Ampex, Toshiba, Matsushita, JVC, and Sony participated in a technology race that would last two decades. Ultimately, JVC overcame the technical lead of Sony and U.S. pioneers by introducing the first successful products for the home market.

Although there are many reasons for the failure of U.S. firms to win this innovation race, at least one reason seems to be the role of middle management in Japan. In 1970, engineers at all the major firms had available to them the technology needed in a consumer-oriented VTR, and top management at each firm seemingly had made a strong commitment to the product. Several alternatives had already met disaster before JVC's VHS was introduced. They had failed to balance market needs with the capabilities of the new technology.

Within JVC, however, middle management made a difference in three ways. First, from the beginning, there was a close connection between the VTR design and manufacturing sections at JVC. In the early stages, the product was manufactured in a special unit of the R&D department. Later, when a separate video division was established, design and production remained co-located. Managers in the two functions therefore began to think alike, according to the same mindset, transcending the traditional engineering/manufacturing dichotomy that plagued U.S. firms during the period (and in many instances still does).

Second and partly as a result of this inherent cross-functionalism, the manager in charge of VTR development, Yuma Shiraishi, understood the crucial trade-offs between design and production costs. He articulated priorities to his engineers in a way that blended price and performance, and as the project grew, he added personnel with expertise in marketing to the team. He defined his team's mission as follows: to figure out what consumers wanted and to match these needs with appropriate technical solutions. The team came to see this as a matrix, and this framework translated a rather lofty vision into concrete considerations of customer needs and specific alternatives. The same conceptual scheme was also a source of rationale used by Shiraishi with top management in his attempts to maintain a consistent flow of resources.

Third, even when senior executives began to withdraw support, Shiraishi had enough confidence and surplus resources to continue to nourish the project's development. The video division at JVC was operating at a loss in the early 1970s. Shiraishi kept his efforts to build a prototype hidden from top management until after the prototype looked promising.[5]

Thus, by keeping "one eye" focused on the consumer and simultaneously integrating design and production priorities, Yuma Shiraishi correctly synthesized the need for "reasonable" production costs with the need for attractive product features. Shiraishi used his personal knowledge as justification for acting outside the bounds of official sanction. He also used it in his interactions with top- and operating-level personnel, where it was shared and elaborated. This process established a framework on which to build the organization's knowledge base and thereby contributed to JVC's ability to succeed where others had failed.

Correcting Management Myopia

Part of the reason that middle management's information links are important as supplements to those provided by top- and operating-level management is simple communication. There are stark differences in status between the top and bottom of an organization, and bad news from operations about the actions of customers, competitors, suppliers, or operations is often kept from senior executives.

No matter how hard they try, for example, it is often difficult for top managers to get "ordinary" people to be frank with them. This applies to customers and suppliers as well as employees. It is easy to observe this in conversations at conventions or trade shows. Typically, the dialogue between the chief executive and the customer is polite and light-hearted. Everybody is smiling. Even if they have complaints, most customers will hold them for the sales manager because no one wants to offend a president who could be quite powerful and who probably cannot solve the problem anyway. Often then, the chief executive is the last to know when something goes wrong.

Competitors are another outside contact residing almost exclusively in the domain of middle managers. Law forbids most top managers from having detailed discussion with rivals, and although operating personnel may encounter the competition, they are rarely in a position to appreciate the implications of what they see. Thus, although top managers can track major trends, monitoring competitor tactics falls on the shoulders of middle managers. How they color a rival's behavior often determines whether top management sees the need for change.

The president of a restaurant equipment company, for example, had based his company's strategy on the idea that they were "the Cadillac of the industry." His kick-off speech at sales meetings always emphasized the need to sell product and engineering quality and to soft-pedal the high prices that went with them. Over a period of twelve months, sales growth began to taper off, and the firm lost a number of large contracts to competitors. Each time a major contract was lost, the marketing manager provided the president with copies of memos documenting the unfavorable price position of the firm's products. These became the subject of frequent phone conversations in which the manager reinforced pricing as a threat.

Gradually, the president began to see the issue, though he steadfastly refused to acknowledge the need to compete on price. Then, the sales meeting speech changed, and references to the Cadillac strategy were dropped. Instead, the president described his vision as "high quality, high customer value." The middle manager's links to the competitive arena had changed the vision in important respects, perhaps without the president ever realizing where the new vision came from.

Many top managers go to great efforts to avoid the potential myopia that arises from their social position. No one wants to be the "emperor who has no clothes." Don Peterson, formerly chief executive of Ford Motor Company, shook hands and spoke with every single Ford employee in the process of communicating his message, "Quality is Job One." But people censor themselves in the presence of power, and even if a few individuals are direct, the picture is still likely to be distorted. Thus, middle management's synthesis becomes key to creating a valid strategic mindset.

When Core Capabilities Become Core Rigidities

Middle managers are people, and like anyone else, they enjoy the fruits of their labor, including the status and perks that accompany their position. More important, they often have the political power to defend such perks. Interestingly, it is middle managers' capability-producing knowledge that is the source of their power. As managers at the top come to depend on them, middle managers are sometimes prone to manipulate situations to make their units look good and to protect their turf. William Guth and Ian MacMillan studied this phenomena and found that when threatened, middle managers tended to "drag their feet" and sometimes even to sabotage the company strategy.[6]

This is the paradox of middle management's role in organization capability. They are in a unique position to accumulate knowledge vital to the organization's strategic interests. But when they feel their self-interests threatened, this same knowledge gives them the power to undermine the legitimate need for change. In short, knowledge is power, and since keeping it is easier than getting it, power reinforces itself.

Dorothy Leonard-Barton observed that for every core organizational capability there is a potential "core rigidity."[7] Over time, organizations become vested in a particular mindset. Reliance on a specialized set of people and other assets creates a power base from which capabilities are perpetuated even if they are no longer appropriate. Perpetuation of existing capabilities, in turn, typically stands in the way of accumulating new ones. Ironically, then, capabilities have a tendency to become rigidities, unless managers pay attention to the dynamics of their situation and the organizational impediments to learning.

One of the worst aspects of the tendency toward rigidity is that it is often difficult to tell whether resistance to change on the part of middle managers represents self-serving behavior or a genuine desire to protect the organization.

Recently, the manager in charge of corporate information systems for a diversified aerospace company had implemented two successive waves of downsizing, reluctantly reducing staff over two years from over 280 to just under 160. All the while, feedback from system users indicated the need for more advanced systems and better information. The manager was unusually loyal, and his integrity had earned him the respect of both peers and subordinates. When he resisted a third wave of 20 percent staff reductions, however, his concerns were interpreted by senior management as protection of turf. The manager lost influence and became tagged as a "change resister."

Who is "right" in a particular situation is not the point. One can endlessly debate the value of a specific resource. The more important issue for the success of the organization is whether the behavior is an expression of core rigidity or dynamic capability. Recognizing the difference and encouraging the latter are the key challenges in managing organizational learning. Beginning in Chapter Four, we suggest a specific set of middle manager behaviors as a basis for resisting rigidity.

Before doing so, however, the next chapter closes the context-setting part of the book by knitting together the lessons of Chapters One and Two. In particular, Chapter Three shows how the pursuit of capability-based advantage through restructuring has been frustrated by outdated views of middle management work.

Summary

The new capability-based model of competition puts managerial knowledge at the forefront of competitive advantage. The knowledge of individual middle managers may become crucial in recognizing an organization's shortcomings and in broadening its capacity to change. Perhaps even more important, the middle manager's centrality in the information network creates the potential for them to become a driving force in organizational learning. Realizing this potential, however, demands a new set of management expectations.

Chapter Three

Realigning Resources and Talent

The Challenge of Organizational Restructuring

Restructuring surely has arrived among the business panaceas of the 1990s. Unprecedented levels of competition, new technologies, and consumer demands have forced firms to rethink their priorities and realign their organizational resources. As the case below illustrates, however, restructuring has been seen primarily as an opportunity to increase efficiency and reduce costs.

Losing the Forest for the Trees

Several years ago, a large mail-order firm used the advent of automated information and communications technology as an opportunity to "restructure" its sales and customer service departments. Originally the technology was acquired with the idea that it would allow the firm to offer better service, "to be more responsive to customers's needs." The initial restructuring was initiated with this objective.

Quickly, however, top management saw the potential of the technology for lowering operating costs. This was first manifested in the elimination of several managerial and supervisory positions. As one key manager told us, "Since the computer created a detailed record of each employee's activities, the need for direct supervision was greatly curtailed." In addition, customer calls could now be screened and directed for appropriate handling through an automated PBX system.

The restructuring effort continued in a direction not initially anticipated. The technology was used to differentiate routine customer ordering from more complex inquiries, and the firm replaced many of its relatively expensive "seasoned" representatives with lower-paid "order takers." More complex inquiries were directed to what was now a relatively small group of experienced and knowledgeable customer service representatives.

As predicted, lowering the overall head count did reduce operating costs. Less expected, however, was that customer satisfaction also declined. Those with complaints or product questions were put on hold, often for several minutes, before they could speak to a real person. Most telling, over a six-month period, sales declined by almost 5 percent as customers who could not get their product questions easily answered put off ordering.

Necessity Versus Advantage

Unfortunately, what happened in this case is all too common within the organizational restructuring movement. What begins as a sincere attempt to enhance organizational capability winds up damaging it. The problem is that, in the course of restructuring, firms lose sight of the distinction between what is a *strategic necessity* and what is a *source of competitive advantage*. Though a certain price parity with respect to rivals is needed, merely lowering costs is unlikely to improve long-term competitiveness. Effective restructuring must do more than lower costs. It must realign organizational resources, including managerial talent, in a way that provides the firm with new capabilities—capabilities aimed at innovation and responsiveness to customers.

Fortunately, in the mail-order firm described above, this realignment was brought about by a middle manager who had detailed operating knowledge and customer contact. One day, a long-time customer told the manager that he had almost stopped buying from the firm because it had become more and more difficult to get the kind of technical product information he needed to make purchase decisions. The manager realized that the system simply wasn't working.

What happened next is telling. The manager brought the problem up at a staff meeting that included several of the firm's top-level executives. To his dismay, the issue was discounted and quickly dismissed.

At the operating level, however, the problem didn't go away, and after several similar incidents the manager, together with several senior customer service representatives, began brainstorming for a solution.

> The key was to come up with something that did not alarm senior management. Tom [the division president] judged our entire operation in terms of costs. . . . A related problem was the turnover and lack of commitment among our sales people. The job had become a dead end. Operators were merely order takers—very low paid. Most just used the job as a "fill-in" while waiting for something else. . . . I began talking to these folks about their jobs and any ideas they had for improving the operation. Interestingly, what seemed most relevant to them was the stress they felt from not being able to answer legitimate customer inquiries.

Based on these conversations, a series of informal training sessions was initiated to provide sales operators with specific product information. The sessions were a big success. People attended on their own time, and the effect was to raise morale immediately. "Over time we saw sales people thriving with expanded job responsibilities and we started giving them more and more latitude." The system continued to be refined as operators gained experience and learned "what worked and what didn't."

Within the department, the operators began to be called account managers. They were encouraged to give out their personal extensions and to take a proactive role in managing selected accounts. Predictably, as people became more knowledgeable and took on more responsibility, they began to seek greater rewards and recognition. In response, the manager began making promises that he knew "he might not be able to keep." These assurances pushed the process to the next stage because they made it necessary to seek formal approval for the new account management system.

The manager began documenting the results and eventually developed a convincing case for the evolving system. Ultimately, to deliver on his promises, he brought the new arrangement to the attention of upper management. "It was after the fact. We'd been doing things differently for almost six months. They [top management] were skeptical and a little put off, but over time the system's been a great success. Our costs really haven't risen much, and our customer satisfaction and sales volume are at record levels."

The story illustrates the strategic importance of middle managers to the restructuring process. The manager in this case used strategic bits of information to forge a set of arrangements that, in addition to maintaining efficiency, created a competitive advantage in the form of unrivaled customer service.

The Paradox of Restructuring

There is, then, a subtle irony or paradox underlying the restructuring process. Redundancies and inefficiencies are often uncovered, and layoffs may have their place. At its heart, however, restructuring is about enhancing organizational capabilities, and when people go, so do their individual skills and competencies. In the case just described, for example, an investment in training was required merely to replace skills that were lost when experienced customer service representatives were let go.

Perhaps more critical than individual skills, however, are organization-level capabilities. These represent the firm's ability to exploit individual technologies and skills by coordinating and deploying them in an overall strategy. Those in the middle are central to this process: they provide critical linkages between various aspects of the firm's operations and between operations, top management, customers, and suppliers.

Such capabilities can be destroyed when middle managers—who are at the very heart of the firm's technical and social networks—disappear. Once lost, these organization-level competencies are usually irrecoverable.

Restructuring's Misplaced Emphasis on Middle Management

The basic paradox of restructuring and its implications have often been clouded by outmoded thinking surrounding the role of middle management. As firms restructure around horizontal processes and operational empowerment, those in the middle are often viewed as dead wood. They are seen as representing an obsolete vertical chain of command and as a source of delay, inhibiting the new priority of responsiveness.

In many cases then, restructuring has resulted in the wholesale elimination of middle managers. Consider the following statistics. Between 1987 and 1991 more than five million white-collar jobs were eliminated in Fortune 1000 firms. Further, although it makes up less than 5 percent of the work force, middle management accounts for roughly 20 percent of all job losses since 1988.[1] Almost half of the 870 companies responding to a 1993 American Management Association survey said they had reduced middle management employment, and two-thirds of those said it was for the second year in a row. In all, fully 72 percent of surveyed firms reported having proportionately fewer middle managers than five years ago, and most see the trend as continuing.[2]

There is, however, growing evidence to suggest that, when focused on the elimination of middle management, restructuring can result in the erosion of competitive advantage and can risk serious strategic and economic damage to the firm. Kodak, for example, slashed 12,000 positions between 1988 and 1992—many of them middle managers. There were no lasting performance improvements, however. Instead, innovation and creativity declined, and the company fell behind in the crucial race for new products.[3] But is Kodak typical?

Clearly, their approach is. In an award-winning article, Wayne Cascio, a human resources professor at the University of Colorado's Denver campus, notes that "nearly a million managers earning more than $40,000 a year lost their jobs in 1991, and in fact, each year for the past three years, between one and two million middle managers were laid off".[4] Cascio attributes the layoffs to a tantalizing logic:

> Hence, cutting costs by cutting people appears to be a natural strategy. . . . Carving out entire echelons of middle-level managers certainly does reduce overhead, and trims the number of layers in the organizational hierarchy. In theory this should lead to less bureaucracy and faster decision making. . . . With fewer layers of middle managers to "filter" information, communications should be

smoother and more accurate, entrepreneurship should flourish, and productivity should climb.

The evidence, however, suggests the results are often disappointing. A Wyatt Company study, for example, found that of 1,005 firms, only 210, or 21 percent, reported satisfactory improvements in profitability. Another study, which tracked the stock prices of sixteen companies that downsized between 1982 and 1988, found that on the day that cuts were announced stock prices generally increased, but the increases were followed shortly by a long, slow slide. Two years later, ten of the sixteen stocks were trading between 17 and 48 percent below the market and twelve were below comparable firms in their industry by 5 to 45 percent.[5]

As more evidence, an in-depth case study of a defense contractor by Mohamed Hussein, an accounting professor at the University of Connecticut, found that eliminating a layer of management and cutting staff did indeed result in an increase in the level of sales per employee. While this demonstrates the alluring certainty of downsizing, the company also experienced an *increase* in costs and expenses as a percentage of total sales![6] The case is consistent with a study of 1,468 restructured companies surveyed by the Society for Human Resource Management and reported in Cascio's article: more than half reported that employee productivity either stayed the same or deteriorated after the layoffs.[7]

Others have reached similar conclusions. When the Conference Board asked member firms to provide evidence that cutbacks in middle management had a favorable impact on the bottom line, "only 23 of 70 firms were able to claim that all or most of their objectives had been met."[8] Thus, there is an abundance of evidence that downsizing, by itself, is not a panacea. Six months to a year after downsizing, key indicators often do not improve. Expense ratios, profits, return on investment to shareholders, and stock prices have all been found to suffer following the elimination of middle management.[9]

Realizing the Promise of Restructuring

There are many potential explanations for the unmet expectations of restructuring. Our explanation is that in their enthusiasm to reduce costs, firms get caught up in the idea that middle management is the enemy. Instead of harnessing the experience and capability of key managers, firms have simply fired them, often with disastrous results.

Realizing the promise of restructuring depends on a realistic picture of middle management's role in today's business environment. Middle managers have always served both operational and strategic functions within organizations. In traditional hierarchical organizations, however, their operational responsibilities have been so predominant that their potential strategic contributions have gone unnoticed.

All this changes, however, in the context of the restructured firm. Although restructuring is often perceived as a death knell for middle managers, when pursued appropriately it actually enhances their value. Fundamentally, restructuring represents a move away from the traditional top-down, command-and-control model of organization toward a more decentralized, "process-centered" orientation where power emanates from the middle. Ironically then, as layers of middle managers are reduced and formal line authority curtailed, the strategic influence of those in the middle becomes more evident.

At present, however, there seems to be little support for, or even understanding of, middle management's strategic value within most organizations. More times than not middle managers are seen as barriers to change, more a part of the problem than the solution. In many cases top managers don't know what they should expect from their middle managers, and middle managers themselves often misinterpret their own job responsibilities.

Summary

Organizational restructuring has become a common response to the increased competitiveness inherent in today's economy. More and more, firms are looking to their middles to identify redundant resources and excess costs. In most cases, however, restructuring is conducted with little appreciation for how middle managers link organizational capability with firm strategy. The result? Increased efficiencies are more than outweighed by a loss in capability when middle managers, central figures in the firm's technical and social networks, are eliminated.

To move forward, firms need a better understanding of the essential role of middle managers in creating and sustaining competitive advantage. In Part Two we detail the strategy development process and the unique contributions of middle managers. We introduce and examine four strategic roles. Together, these roles represent a new vision and set of expectations for middle management: a vision that intimately links middle management behavior to a firm's strategic effectiveness.

Part Two

The New Strategic Roles for Middle Managers

Chapter Four

Strategy from the Middle Out

The old model of how organizations made strategy separated strategic thinking from doing. Top managers had *all* the important strategic ideas, which they formulated into plans to be carried out by others. Middle managers were merely conduits, translating plans into action, monitoring and controlling activities to keep things on track. While this command-and-control model of strategy never accurately reflected what really went on, its apparent fit with the hierarchies of the past caused it to dominate our thinking about strategy for decades. Middle managers, it was thought, lacked a strategic perspective because they lived their lives within the functional corridors of an organization's hierarchy.

Today, most observers would agree that the old division of work no longer applies. Indeed, the overly rational, command-and-control model has been abandoned in favor of learning theory as a basis for describing how strategy is created.[1] Instead of using the terms *formulation* and *implementation* to describe the strategic division of work, a more holistic term—*formation*—has been adopted to describe the process. That is, strategy is seen to form out of the pattern of actions and decisions taken by many members of the organization over time.

Chapter Two described the role organizational capabilities play in achieving competitive advantage. From this perspective, strategy formation can be viewed as *the organizational learning processes associated with the accumulation and deployment of organizational capabilities.* This chapter highlights the centrality of middle managers in strategy formation and begins to describe their specific contributions.

From Turf Battles to Strategic Campaigns

Several years ago, we worked with a consumer products firm instituting a team-based approach to product development. Prior to this change, the firm's activities were fragmented, housed in separate departments that had little or no communication with one another. New product development began in the R&D department. Promising new product concepts were brought directly to top management who made "go" or "no go" decisions. From R&D, concepts were brought on line, sequentially proceeding from one department to the next. Provided with formal documentation and perhaps a prototype, individual functions (for example, production engineering, graphics, packaging, manufacturing, and marketing) added their unique contributions, all the while interpreting and redefining the original concept.

Not surprisingly, this process created conflicts across departments and ultimately delayed the introduction of the firm's products. Miscommunication and imperfect coordination caused errors to be compounded as projects moved from one activity to the next. Sooner or later (usually later), these problems became apparent and conflicts erupted, as it was never clear where responsibility fell. To make matters worse, this functional sequencing reduced middle managers to defenders of their "turf." Rather than attempting to solve problems, middle managers typically took a defensive posture, often declaring, "Hey, my guys did what they were supposed to!"

While the story so far illustrates many of the problems inherent to hierarchical organizations, an episode that occurred as the firm began experimenting with the team-based approach provides another example of the potential strategic value of middle management. A marketing specialist assigned to one of the first new product teams came to his manager about a conflict that had emerged over a procedural issue the team had been unable to resolve. Almost as a knee-jerk reaction the manager adopted a functional perspective, steadfastly defending the way things had always been done. After some debate and "arm twisting," the manager agreed to meet with the team in support of his employee.

> I began to see the problems the issue was creating. Unfortunately there didn't appear to be a straightforward solution and no one, including myself, had enough information to formulate a good

alternative. I left the meeting having defended my employee but knowing the problem wasn't solved. The next day while discussing unrelated issues over lunch with my boss [the division president] I developed a new insight into the team's problem. I went back to the team and coached them through a tentative arrangement. I really didn't have any formal authority, most of these people didn't work for me, and some I hardly knew.

After a few weeks the manager asked the marketing specialist how things were going. To his surprise, the employee reported that the agreed-upon arrangement had failed but that the group had developed an alternative solution that seemed to be working fine. The only problem was that the new solution required "a fair degree of subterfuge. If engineering gets wind of it, all hell will break loose."

At that point I was anxious to see what the group had come up with. I met with the team again and suddenly realized that the new arrangement, while very creative, could jeopardize our product certification. Feeling more than a little responsible, I went to fill in Jack [the engineering manager]. Fortunately, the issue became a non-event. Regulations had changed and as it turned out the solution the team had developed was perfect!

A short time later the marketing manager presented the team's solution as a formal proposal to upper management for a new product development process. Today this administrative innovation represents the cornerstone of the firm's new product strategy. It has significantly shortened the product development cycle and dramatically strengthened the firm's creative capability. Successful new product introductions have increased, and the firm has begun to develop a reputation as an innovative leader in its industry.

Strategy from the Middle Out

What is perhaps most revealing about this case is what it says about how strategies actually develop. This is not a story about top managers who have all the answers. In fact, top management remained largely oblivious to the new process until it had fully developed. Operating personnel were the first to recognize the need for change. It was a middle manager, however, who was able to provide the knowledge and perspective to facilitate a successful solution.

There is an important lesson here. Strategies don't develop full-blown from the minds of top managers or anyone else. Rather, strategies develop over time through successive iterations of decisions and actions. Most of the time nobody even recognizes the strategic implications of what is going on until much later. In this case, top management had encouraged the formation of teams as a way to smooth out the product development process. But they really did not understand the details involved, nor did they anticipate the dramatic effect the realignment would have on the firm's strategy.

Honda's entry into the U.S. motorcycle industry in the early 1960s provides another case in point.[2] At the outset, Honda merely wanted to sell its excess inventory of "large" motorcycles (250cc). The firm learned, however, that American road bikes were typically even larger than what Honda offered, and their product proved unreliable under the driving conditions in the U.S. market. Honda's managers had brought much smaller "Cub 50" cycles for commuting purposes. One day a Sears representative saw two of Honda's managers riding around Los Angeles and queried them about the bike. After several conversations among themselves the Honda middle managers recommended to headquarters that Cub 50s be exported. Only then did Honda have the idea to sell its smallest bikes in the United States, and the result was nothing short of a revolution in the industry.

Strategy, then, means taking action, experimenting, and learning from the results, or what the Japanese call "adaptive persistence." This learning requires listening and communication across levels and boundaries of the organization. In the Honda case, the Sears representative contacted the managers he saw in Los Angeles. The salesmen, blinded by their mission to market large motorcycles, could have easily dismissed the opportunity. Instead, they apparently recognized the strategic potential and presented the idea to their superiors in Japan. For their part, the executives in Japan might have questioned how this helped with the inventory problem. Instead, they seized the opportunity, and within a few years Honda became the largest seller of motorcycles in the United States.

The Honda case provides a good example of combining what Henry Mintzberg refers to as the deliberate and emergent elements of strategy.[3] Certainly, the executives at Honda took some deliberate steps to sell motorcycles in North America. What emerged, however, was in no way envisioned or planned. The key to success was a strategically nimble organization, one capable of listening, learning, and effectively adapting to unanticipated events and results.

Experimentation is essential to this process. Multiple small-scale demonstration projects represent more than just side bets. They are the basis by which the firm develops new capabilities. Moreover, they cannot be judged in the short term, nor in terms of direct payoffs. Their true value emerges most often serendipitously, in ways never imagined.

In science, for example, the microwave oven was developed after a researcher mistakenly left his lunch on a counter where a communications experiment was taking place. The development of Teflon and countless other scientific and commercial innovations have similar roots. A similar phenomenon takes place in strategy making. The decision to institute product development teams discussed above was seen merely as an efficiency move. No one anticipated that this administrative change would result in a process innovation and provide the firm with a capability that would dramatically reposition the firm in its industry.

Recognizing that strategy has more to do with learning than planning holds powerful implications for both top- and middle-level managers. In today's complex and turbulent business environments, top managers increasingly employ what James Brian Quinn refers to as "logical incrementalism."[4] Too much is unknown at any one time for top management to formulate a detailed plan that can simply be implemented by others. More accurately, top managers provide a "logic" that guides the continual readjustment and rethinking of strategy as events unfold. Rather than trying to be clairvoyant, effective top managers recognize the need for organizational flexibility. They build organizations that are highly sensitive to emerging developments. And since no single sensor can grasp the full complexity of the environment, they encourage a wide variety of inputs and perspectives.

Middle Management's Strategic Involvement and Organizational Performance

In 1989, we conducted our first study to formally examine how middle managers fit into the strategy process.[5] Figure 4.1 summarizes our hypotheses concerning two possible ways middle management involvement in strategy might affect organizational performance. The traditional view (Path A) was that their involvement was needed to facilitate smooth implementation. Getting middle managers involved ensured that they understood the plan and were committed to its execution. An alternative explanation, not usually given much credence in the classical model, was that middle management involvement might actually be substantive and lead to better strategic decisions (Path B).

To examine this issue, we identified five steps that were typically found in strategic decision making[6] and asked a selected set of middle managers from twenty firms to assess their level of participation in each step. Separately, we measured their organization's financial performance. Our findings were surprising: enhanced firm performance was associated with middle management involvement in (1) proposing objectives, (2) generating options, and (3) evaluating options. Improved firm performance was not associated with middle management involvement in (4) developing details or (5) taking necessary actions. In other words, Path B, by which middle management involvement in strategy substantively improves the quality of strate-

Figure 4.1. Middle Management Involvement in Strategy and Organizational Performance.

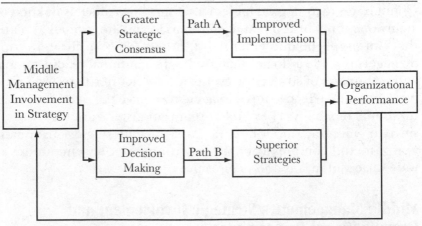

Source: Wooldridge and Floyd, "The Strategy Process, Middle Management Involvement, and Organizational Performance," *Strategic Management Journal,* 1990, *11,* 231–241. Reprinted by permission.

gic decisions, appeared to account for improved firm performance.[7]

In subsequent studies, we interviewed and surveyed top and middle-level managers from over seventy-five firms with similar results. While a high level of involvement in developing the details of strategy and taking necessary actions was generally reported, these forms of participation were relatively uniform across firms and therefore did not separate high-performance firms from the rest of the pack. We repeatedly found that high-performance firms regularly involve their middle managers in the substantive development of organizational strategy. As our work has continued, we have focused on the reasons underlying this relationship and have identified four distinct middle management roles in strategy.

Four Middle Management Roles in Strategy

Understanding the nature of dynamic capability discussed in Chapter Two is the key to appreciating how middle managers influence the quality of strategy. This is not to underestimate the role of top or operating managers. Top managers instill the organization with a sense of direction, a vision of where the firm is headed. This constancy of purpose acts as a force that coordinates diverse activities and ensures that the organization continues to move toward its goals. Operating-level personnel, on the other hand, actualize and refine organizational capabilities. This is where the work of the organization gets accomplished, where "the rubber meets the road." Operating-level managers are connected with relevant technologies, processes, and capacities. Here, there is a keen sense of requirements and possibilities.

Positioned between these two, middle managers are centrally located at the interplay between strategic purpose and organizational action. Over time, they develop a rich knowledge base that combines strategic awareness with operating experience. Through dialogues with both top and bottom, they influence strategy in both upward and downward directions. In so doing, they may advance the current strategic direction or work to change it. In short, people in the middle are in the best position to fit strategic-level data with operating-level data and to influence the evolving strategic context. They are truly the linchpins of effective strategy making.

Recognizing this allowed us to develop a framework detailing the ways middle managers contribute to strategy and advance the firm's dynamic capability. The framework presented in Figure 4.2 combines upward and downward influence with behaviors that integrate and support strategies on one hand and diverge from official strategy on the other. The interaction of direction of influence and its impact on existing strategy leads to a description of four strategic middle management roles: championing strategic alternatives, synthesizing information, facilitating adaptability, and implementing deliberate strategy. As the figure shows, while each role is distinguished by its upward or downward influence, common among all the roles is the need for effective lateral influence across the organization.

Championing Strategic Alternatives

Working in the organizational zone between strategy and operations, middle managers are uniquely qualified to bring entrepreneurial and innovative proposals to top management's attention. In the consumer products firm discussed earlier, it was a middle manager who ultimately championed the innovative administrative arrangement and gained top management approval. Presenting this idea to top management represented the culmination of a long sequence of activities. First, the manager acted as an initial screen, listening to various proposals and counterproposals from the team. Because he lacked formal authority, however, his success at this stage depended on his ability to get informal cooperation and buy-in from the team's members. The team then experimented with the new arrangement,

Figure 4.2. Middle Management's Four Strategic Roles.

| | | Nature of Contribution | |
		Divergent	Integrative
Upward Influence	Lateral	Championing	Synthesizing
Downward Influence		Facilitating	Implementing

Source: Wooldridge and Floyd, "Middle Management Involvement in Strategy and Its Association with Strategic Type: A Research Note," *Strategic Management Journal,* 1992, *13,* 153–167. Reprinted by permission.

modifying it until a feasible solution emerged. Only then did the manager have a credible proposal to advocate to top management.

In other contexts, managers use these same processes to select and nurture new business opportunities from the many suggested at operating levels. Having selected a proposal, managers nurture these ideas by providing seed resources and "cover" that allow their unit to gain experience, establish feasibility, and demonstrate potential.

Synthesizing Information

Middle management's position between strategy and operations also provides a unique perspective for making sense of the diverse array of information coming from both inside and outside the organization. Thus, in addition to championing strategic proposals, middle managers frequently supply information to top management, saturating the information with meaning through personal evaluation and explicit advice giving. Events are reported as "threats" or "opportunities," and these seemingly innocent labels are a powerful influence on how superiors see their situation.

Effective middle managers often use this role to promote their own agendas. Indeed, synthesizing may be a precursor to championing a full-blown proposal. In *Managing the Resource Allocation Process*,[8] for example, Harvard's Joseph Bower describes middle managers who framed information and "managed" top management perceptions for years until the timing was right to champion a pet project as a new business venture.

In short, middle managers are often able to control or at least influence top management perceptions by framing information in certain ways. They have been called information filters or "uncertainty absorbers,"[9] but the process is not necessarily conscious or manipulative. In the end, this role can be crucial in encouraging cautious top managers to take needed risks.

Facilitating Adaptability

Middle managers make their organizations more flexible and stimulate behavior that diverges from official expectation. Based on our interviews with managers, we compare this role with the flexible, accordion-like structure between the two sections of a reticulated passenger bus. The shape and composition of the accordion overcomes the rigidities of the vehicle, while at the same time ensuring that the front and back go in the same direction.

In her clinical analysis of a large computer manufacturer, Rosabeth Kanter describes the efforts of middle managers who sheltered and encouraged an employee involvement program in the midst of an emotional, top-down redesign of production processes.[10] The middle managers created an environment in which fears about the change could surface and be brought into the discussion. Participation helped the organization adapt to the new work processes, but the process diverged completely from top management's original intention. Without middle management's effort to facilitate change, however, top management's reengineering effort would have met considerably more resistance and could have failed.

Returning to our consumer products firm, before the intervention of the marketing manager, the product development team had reached a point of impasse. They were out of ideas and frustrated. The team concept might easily have been shelved had the initial conflict escalated. The manager, however, coached them through this period, providing key information and, equally important, encouragement. Merely meeting with the group lent support and reassured team members that the issue had legitimacy. Thus, although middle managers are stereotyped as change resisters, when they encourage cross-functional problem solving, experimentation, and learning, they may be closer to what Kanter describes as "change masters."[11]

Implementing Deliberate Strategy

In championing, synthesizing, and facilitating, middle managers go beyond or even ignore the plans embedded in top management's deliberate strategy. Their most commonly recognized strategic role, however, is the implementation of top management's intentions. Here, the strategic contribution rests on middle managers' efforts to deploy existing resources efficiently and effectively. Reports suggest a widening gap between intentions and implementation, however, and the cause is often attributed to middle management obstinacy. Our research suggests another explanation.

Implementation is commonly perceived as a mechanical process in which plans are deduced and carried out from a master strategy conceived by top management. The reality is more complex. Even in fairly stable situations (which are rare in today's business world), priorities must be revised as conditions evolve and new information presents itself. Implementation, therefore, is best characterized as an ongoing series of interventions that are only partly anticipated in top management plans and that adjust the direction to suit emergent events.

In short, the conception that top managers formulate strategy while middle managers merely carry it out is not only unrealistic but is also self-defeating. Effective implementation requires that middle managers have a firm understanding of the strategic rationale behind the plan, in addition to specific directives. Experience tells us that such understanding results from broad participation in the strategic process. Middle managers' effectiveness in implementing strategy is thus directly related to their involvement in other roles. The "implementation gap" reflects a broader chasm between senior management's perception of implementation and what middle managers must know to get the job done.

Research Evidence on Middle Management's Strategic Roles and Organizational Performance

In 1991, we conducted a large-scale statistical study involving hundreds of middle managers across twenty-five organizations. Our results uncovered three convincing patterns.[12] First, in organizations whose strategy depended on product innovation, exploiting new market opportunities, and maintaining flexible organizational priorities, we found significantly higher levels of middle management championing and facilitating, when compared to organizations whose strategy relied on narrow product lines and organizational efficiency. Since core capability in innovating firms is related to the discovery of new business opportunity and operational flexibility, this result suggested the centrality of middle management.

Second, we found certain middle managers to be greater champions than others. In particular, managers in marketing, sales, purchasing, and R&D engaged in significantly more championing behavior than managers from other functions. Ideas arose most often from interactions with customers, suppliers, and technologies, and we found championing highest where such exposure was most likely. Not only was innovative ability related to middle management championing and facilitating, then, but these behaviors were concentrated in certain positions. In other words, middle managers appeared to utilize strategically important knowledge in ways that fostered the development of new strategies.

These results supported our argument of middle management's importance to strategy and showed that some middle management positions were more important than others. To establish a link between middle management and competitive advantage, however, we needed to determine whether such behavior actually led to improved economic performance. Based on logic and the available anecdotal evidence, however, we did not expect a simple linear relationship. In fact, this appeared to be a case where more is not necessarily better.

Rather than simply engaging in more of each behavior, successful strategy demands variety. A similar notion was advanced by Stuart Hart and Catherine Banbury, who showed in a survey of top managers that firms that combined a diverse mix of strategy-making skills enjoyed enhanced capability and organizational performance.[13] These skills included everything from formal planning procedures to informal experimentation and even creating a "dream" about the company's future. Such skills and the behaviors associated with them are not likely to be distributed evenly throughout organizations. The successful formal planner, for example, is not likely to be the best "dreamer."

Similarly, middle managers are likely to differ widely in their ability and willingness to assume a strategic role at a particular point in time. More important, the relevance and usefulness of particular managers assuming a given role rests heavily on the strategic situation. As a result, one would expect considerable variation in the types of middle management strategic behavior in firms that successfully develop core capability.

To test this expectation, we asked top managers to assess the financial performance of their organizations. We then examined whether performance was associated with a statistical measure of variation in middle management behavior. The results were convincing. We found strong relationships[14] between variation in the performance of the strategic roles and the economic performance of the firms. Thus we had the first evidence supporting the proposition that middle managers are pivotal in the creation of the organizational capabilities that form the basis of competitive advantage.[15] In short, not all middle managers should influence strategy equally, and managers should expect their own influence to vary over time.

Middle Management Roles and Negative Stereotypes

Though generally recognized, the activities associated with the four roles are often viewed negatively by top-level and even middle-level managers. Our conversations with top managers reveal that the strategic roles are misunderstood, almost always nonsanctioned, often discouraged, and considered secondary. As with most stereotypes, there is a grain of truth in the negative perceptions.

Nonetheless, the stereotypes associated with the four roles (see Figure 4.3) stem from the misunderstanding of middle management work described in Chapter One. That is, where top managers expect middle managers to act as administrators or bureaucrats they are likely to react negatively to upward and divergent behavior.

Middle Manager as Politician

The champion's potential contribution is not always appreciated. One top manager described middle management championing as an "earned right," reserved only for a few people in recognition of many years of "credible service." Similarly, many middle managers in our interviews observed that championing meant "spending currency" with top managers. It was pursued sparingly, as an exception. Just as telling, some middle managers felt their real influence was minimal but that championing was an important means of showing support for the ideas of subordinates.

Figure 4.3. Four Negative Stereotypes.

| | Nature of Contribution | |
	Divergent	Integrative
Upward Influence	The Politician	The Spin Doctor
Downward Influence	The Subversive	The Drone

These comments suggest that middle managers are often seen as the representative of their subunit and that influence is achieved from accumulating a sufficient number of "chips" with senior managers. As with the much maligned influence peddler in Washington, middle managers are seen as bringing forth their pet projects. Too often, the assumption is that there is a hidden agenda, and that somehow, the self-interest of the manager or her subordinate is the real motivation behind a proposal.

Middle Manager as Subversive

The behavior associated with facilitating adaptability is often seen as risky and somewhat subversive. Our case files are full of examples of middle managers diverting resources and hiding experimental programs from top management in order to gain experience and acquire new capabilities. Not surprisingly, many top managers view this role cynically. As one CEO commented to us, "Oh, they've all got their secrets; I guess that's part of the price you pay."

In part, this view results from the fact that the learning gained from experimentation usually shows itself much later. It may be difficult for managers to justify expending today's resources on unknown future benefits. As a result, middle managers are forced to hide things from superiors and to encourage subordinates to work outside the system. In many cases, such activity undermines the formally determined organization goals in the sense that people have removed "their noses from the grindstone." In our experience, however, the flexibility created within the subunit has been crucial in the organization's ability to respond to an ever changing set of circumstances.

Middle Manager as Spin Doctor

The role of middle managers as channels of communication and sources of information is well recognized. Subjective interpretation is inevitable, however, and middle managers are often criticized for "putting their own spin on things." Making sense of organizational reality and putting events into a strategic context are most often seen as top-down processes. Thus, senior managers often go to elaborate efforts using systems such as formal planning to objectify and rationalize middle management input.

Naturally, this approach is the result of the old thinking/doing model of strategy, but the irony is that the more formalized the planning system becomes, the more likely it is to create organizational rigidity. Formal systems are simply unable to respond when a new variable appears on the horizon. By definition, these systems only capture what has been pre-identified as important, and too often it is the least expected event that is most important. Rather than trying to eliminate middle manager bias, senior managers should encourage managers to think, interpret, and synthesize in meaningful strategic terms what they see around them.

Middle Manager as Drone

Along with the view that middle managers should merely report information goes the notion that they should simply *do*. The problem with narrowing middle management's strategic focus strictly to the implementation role, however, is that it makes "doing it" more difficult. We have found consistently that broader middle management involvement in the "thinking" roles (championing and synthesizing) is associated with higher-quality implementation. Few top managers really want middle managers who do not think. Yet what else accounts for the fact that top management so often keeps the real strategy a secret?

Interconnectedness Among the Roles

Before concluding this introduction to middle management's strategic roles, it is important to clarify the interconnectedness among the four roles and to show how they fit into the broader process of strategy making. Like strategic management more generally, middle management's strategic roles have to do with balancing competing organizational needs for stability and change. As described in Part One, conditions throughout much of our recent history were relatively stable and simple. Relationships with suppliers and customers were more or less fixed and easily understood. Technologies were established, and changed only modestly. Traditionally then, it has been appropriate for middle managers (and others) to promote stable and efficient operating systems. It is easy to see, therefore, why the straightforward implementation of established plans is most often viewed as the core strategic role of middle managers.

Today's world, however, is marked by complexity and change. New forms of competition, rapidly changing technologies, and increased customer expectations combine and affect organizations in complex, unpredictable ways. The strategic job of middle management has therefore become increasingly multifaceted. In essence, it has shifted from merely promoting stability to coping with ever increasing complexity. Figure 4.4 provides a simplified illustration of how middle managers add strategic value by adeptly combining the four strategic roles.

Although the reality is more iterative and continuous, one can envision the process as beginning with a synthesis or diagnosis of the strategic context. In performing this role, middle managers gain a sense of the environment's strategic significance. Ambiguities and intricacies facing the firm may raise questions about either "how" the firm's strategy should be discharged or, more fundamentally, "what" changes or additions are needed to strategy. As the figure shows, when the implications revolve largely around the "how" question, facilitating is targeted toward the adaptive implementation of strategy. Alternatively, when environmental complexity raises questions regarding the "what" of strategy, the experimentation and learning supported through middle management's facilitating efforts provide the intelligence necessary to champion new strategic initiatives.

Figure 4.4. Simplified Model of How the Four Roles Combine.

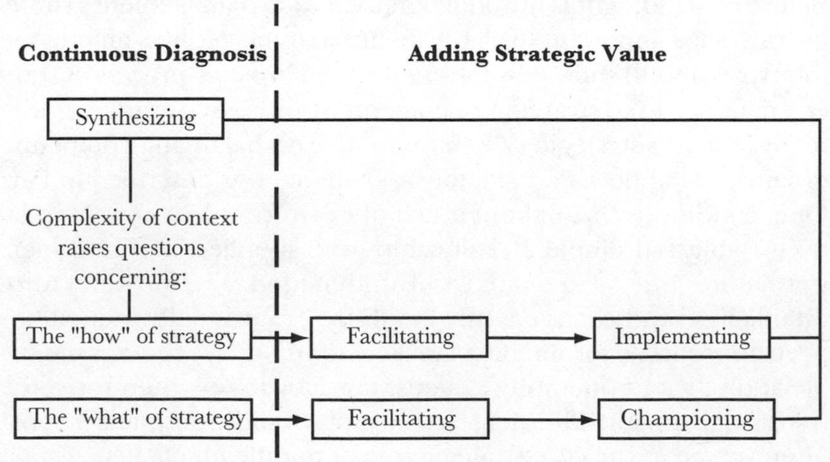

Obviously, the four roles are not as discrete as they appear in Figure 4.4. Nor do they exist outside the context of top management actions. To illustrate this, Figure 4.5 depicts middle management's strategic roles as part of the overall strategic balancing act.

The figure depicts a river[16] of unfolding realized strategies—the flowing water traces the pattern of decisions and actions taken over time by all members of the organization. Emergent decision making from the lower levels (bottom-up strategy) mixes with deliberate decision making from the top (top-down strategy). Middle managers, then, captain a boat floating precariously in the confluence,

Figure 4.5. Middle Management's Strategic Roles and the Strategic Process.

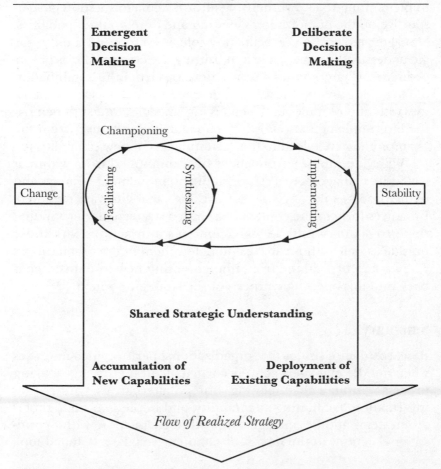

buffeted by the current of both deliberate and emergent forces. Whether the current is rapid or relatively slow, staying afloat among the whirlpools is a continuous challenge.

Middle management's strategic roles therefore have to do with change: understanding the need for change (synthesizing), preparing for it (facilitating), stimulating it (championing), and ultimately, managing the process (implementing). The two revolving orbits in the figure depict the continuous, self-reinforcing and boundaryless nature of the roles. Middle managers synthesize new information, assess the strategic context, and thereby influence the shared strategic understanding within the organization. Synthesizing develops from interactions with top management in the championing role as well as from operational involvement in the facilitating and implementing roles. Synthesizing affords managers a strategic perspective on the organization's existing and developing capabilities. Managers move into the facilitating role when they use their strategic understanding as a guide in nurturing the creative efforts of subordinates. Championing, in turn, develops from the combination of facilitating and synthesizing as managers match nascent capabilities with opportunities in the emerging strategic context. When ratified for implementation by top management, initiatives from the championing cycle lead to the accumulation of new capabilities.

Whether imposed from above or championed from within, it is middle management's responsibility to implement strategy, and in the process, to change the way existing capabilities are deployed. Initiatives form in the context of a shared strategic understanding that grows out of middle management's interactions with those outside as well as those above and below them in the organization. The experience gained from implementing new initiatives feeds back into this ongoing synthesis of the strategic context.

Summary

Research demonstrates that organizational performance improves when middle managers actively participate in the strategy-making process. Through championing strategic alternatives, synthesizing information, facilitating adaptability, and implementing deliberate strategy, middle managers link strategic purpose with organizational action. In the next four chapters we take a detailed look at each of the four roles, further examining their influence on firm strategy. As we will see, effective middle management is about achieving a proper balance among the four roles and matching this to the organization's strategic context.

Chapter Five

Championing
The Discovery and Proposal
of Innovative Initiatives

Championing innovation is rarely considered an "official" part of middle management work. Have you ever seen championing in a job description? Yet, when probed, almost everyone has an example of a middle manager who has been the catalyst behind some important new initiative—be it a new product idea, an administrative innovation, or even a whole new business venture.

Championing is how middle managers promote strategic initiatives to their superiors and in the process diversify the organization's repertoire of capabilities. This role is unique because it centers on a discrete proposal, making it potentially quite visible. Yet, specific behaviors associated with championing are often obscured and unrewarded. The obscurity results in part from the fact that championing is tightly connected to middle management's other activities. That is, championing generally occurs as a consequence of synthesizing, facilitating, and implementing deliberate strategy. Another reason championing goes unnoticed is that it is often confused with other forms of upward influence, many of which serve the narrow self-interests of an individual manager or subunit. Despite the low profile, no role is more fundamental to the innovative deployment of organizational capabilities.

Hallmarks of the Strategic Champion

Middle management championing is the centerpiece of a process that allows firms to evolve and remain viable in a continuously changing business environment. We define championing as: *the persistent and persuasive communication of proposals that either provide the firm with new capabilities or allow the firm to use existing capabilities differently.* Middle management proposals may be in the form of new product concepts, modifications to existing products, initiatives for entirely new businesses, or process improvements that allow the firm to do different things.

Fundamentally, championing is a form of upward influence that involves persuading top management to alter existing priorities—to invest in something that shifts or widens the strategic focus. However, holding sway with those at the top requires laying a foundation of support with others. At a broader level then, effective championing also involves influencing peers, subordinates, customers, and other outside stakeholders.

The kinds of initiatives that bubble up in the organization as a result of middle management championing are integral to organizational innovation. Inventiveness and good ideas are transformed into new strategies through a series of interpersonal exchanges. This is a social influence process by which middle managers mediate between the potential changes inspired at operating levels and top management's strategic intention. In an increasingly equivocal and uncertain environment, organizations rely more and more on this bottom-up approach to strategic change. Championing therefore places middle management at the heart of the firm's regenerative process.

To be effective catalysts of change, strategic champions must feel passionately about the proposals they champion and become deeply involved in their development. As a result of their involvement, they are able to articulate convincingly the details and benefits of their proposals. The list below summarizes the hallmarks of strategic champions and connects them to experience in the other middle management strategic roles.

Hallmarks of Strategic Champions

- Intimate Involvement with Operations (Implementation Experiences)

  Key operating capabilities
  Critical linkages

Key personnel
Credibility and trust

- Deep Understanding of Strategic Logic (Synthesizing Experiences)

  Organizational priorities
  Competitive strategy
  Competitor profiles and products
  Customer requirements and concerns

- Prudent Risk Taking (Facilitating Experiences)

  Selective promotion of divergent ideas
  Perseverance in spite of top management
  Commitment of seed resources
  Provision for safe haven

- Astute Political Sensitivity (Experiences in All Four Roles)

  Dynamics within top management group
  Corridors of indifference
  Coalitions of support

Consider, for example, the case of Tom West as described by Tracy Kidder in "Flying Upside Down."[1] West, a project manager at Data General, orchestrated the development of a new computer that eventually became a mainstay for the company. In the beginning, however, he went forward with little or no top management support. As described by Kidder, West was "a man on a mission."

Intimate Involvement with Operations

Being involved in operations provides the middle manager with knowledge about key personnel and operating capabilities. It provides the basis for judging the feasibility of various initiatives and allows the manager to tap a wide variety of operating talents and expertise.

In developing his new product concept, for example, West "borrowed ideas from anyone who had some to share." He knew the talents and work habits of each one of the thirty-plus product design engineers that worked on Eclipse—the code name Data General adopted for the development project. West had hired many of them, and even though he interacted little with them during the day, he left his door open in the evening. After hours, he would welcome a chat with almost anyone.

In addition to building firsthand knowledge, the middle manager's involvement in operations encourages creative change in others. Hands-on involvement shifts the focus of operating personnel from just getting the job done to a search for improvement. Middle managers who actively participate in solving operating-level problems facilitate critical linkages across activities and people, thereby promoting the development of systemwide solutions. By personally demonstrating the possibility for successful change, involved managers stimulate creative energy in others and enhance the operating core's willingness to develop new capabilities.

> West made the project "definitely more dramatic" than it had to be. He was successful at getting senior [operating-level] people to take a chance and join the project. . . . I'm too old to feel . . . [enthusiastic] about computers now. This would be crashingly dull if I were doing it for someone else. West is interesting. He's the main reason I do what I do.

Deep Understanding of the Strategic Logic

Nurturing and eventually gaining support for a new initiative requires a deep understanding of the firm's strategic situation. Although by 1978 many in Data General recognized the firm would need to respond to recent competitor advances, top management felt little urgency. Existing products were selling well and formal development of a 32-bit machine had begun at a satellite plant in North Carolina. West, however, "believed that whatever its other virtues, the machine that the company engineers in North Carolina were building did not represent a timely solution to the problem."

West's skepticism came from his detailed understanding of both the technology and the customer's needs. Technology was changing rapidly, and 32-bit machines were just one point in a continuous stream of innovations for the industry. Still, the jump to 32-bit machines required customers not only to make new investments but to scrap already substantial stakes in older machines. West began to nurture the notion emerging among engineers of a "schizophrenic" computer that would act as both a 16-bit and 32-bit machine. This "would offer prospective buyers at least the possibility of savings in software development."

Along the way, and well before ever presenting the idea to upper management, West continued to gather strategic information. On a holiday morning in 1978 he secretly visited a competitor's lab, not to imitate but to size up the competition.

> I wasn't really into G2 [competitive intelligence]. VAX was in the public domain, and I wanted to see how bad the damage was. I think I got high when I looked at it and saw how complex and expensive it was. It made me feel good about some of the decisions we've made.

Prudent Risk Taking

To demonstrate feasibility, and to accumulate experience and credibility, middle managers often need to commit resources for new projects prior to gaining top management approval. Within Data General, there had been the usual competition for resources, and the Eclipse group had lost most of their formal support. West's personal commitment was unshaken, however. In fact, he had already launched a big project within his group before getting approval, and getting it started had taken him months. He decided not to abide by top management's official decision and pursued an "indirect" approach with the project.

Most top managers are rightly conservative about supporting new initiatives. Uncontrolled experimentation dilutes resources and takes the organization's eye off the ball. On the other hand, new initiatives represent the firm's future. Thus there is no way around a certain amount of middle management subterfuge. The old adage that it is easier to get forgiveness than permission really does apply.

Our own research has revealed case after case of middle management perseverance in the face of top management ambivalence or even outright resistance. Senior managers often become personally identified with setting a particular course and may be removed from events that challenge their direction. As a result, championing a divergent proposal may require patience: it takes time to prove the idea and build a case. One manager we know provided resources for a burgeoning new product and monitored industry developments for eight years until a key departure in upper management signaled that the initiative's time had come.

Astute Political Sensitivity

How and when to go forward with an idea requires astute political awareness and a keen sense of timing. In nurturing selected initiatives, middle managers "beg, borrow, and steal" assets from wherever and whoever they can. Rarely do successful champions go it alone. This is not only because they need others' resources: they also need their buy-in and political support.

Any new initiative attracts opposition, and the first step in selling new proposals is to build a solid base of support. Perceptive champions focus not on opposing factions but on what Edward Wrapp has called "corridors of comparative indifference."[2] By gaining the commitment of those with little or no initial stake in a proposal, effective managers can move proposals forward almost invisibly, avoiding premature confrontations.

> I tried to low-key the thing. I tried to dull the impression that this was a competing project with North Carolina. I tried to sell it externally as . . . insurance . . . if something went wrong in North Carolina. This was the only way it was gonna live. We had to get the resources without creating a big brouhaha.

In the end, however, champions must take their case to top management. "Bulletproofing" a proposal means being armed with three key elements:

- Solid strategic logic
- Display of feasibility
- Coalition of organizational support

The success of the championing effort is also likely to rest on the manager's understanding of the dynamics within the top management group. How decisions are made, where power is vested, and the positions of each key actor are central considerations in presenting a proposal. Obviously, enlisting one or more top management allies prior to a formal presentation greatly improves the chances of success.

Probably no factor is more important in determining how a proposal will be received by upper management than timing, however. Our research and that of others[3] shows that effective champions are astute at assessing when the timing for a proposal is right. In large part, determining the proper timing rests on two fundamental considerations.

First, prospective champions should consider top management's level of satisfaction with current strategy. Clearly, dissatisfied top managers will be searching for alternative solutions and may be quite interested in what middle managers have to say. When highly satisfied, however, these same executives may see proposals as disruptive and distracting.

Second, astute champions pay attention to the "age" or "life cycle stage" of the strategy. Young strategies, those recently developed and initiated, are likely to be very consistent with current thinking in top management. They will be given time to work, and in these situations, alternative proposals are more likely to be viewed as annoyances. As the strategy ages, however, top management's strategic logic continues to develop, and executives increasingly recognize the limitations and imperfections of a particular course.[4] This provides an opening for those championing new ideas.

In Data General, for example, word got out at a certain point that the competing product development was going to miss its deadline by a wide margin. On learning this, West pressured his group to reach a conclusion on the design's parameters. Then he took the opportunity to begin an aggressive campaign of selling the initiative to top management. He framed his product concept as absolutely essential to the company's future.

In sum, effective strategic champions like Tom West straddle two worlds, blending a working knowledge of operations with a keen awareness of the substance and politics of strategy. Their knowledge at both of these levels makes it possible for them to do the subtle work of encouraging appropriate initiatives and sheltering good ideas, on the one hand, and to carry off the less subtle but equally challenging task of orchestrating formal approvals, on the other.

Upward Influence Versus Championing:
Three Counterproductive Stereotypes

Not every attempt to influence upper management constitutes strategic championing, and our discussions with upper- and middle-level managers have uncovered a great deal of confusion surrounding this role. When asked to provide illustrations of championing, for example, many middle managers describe upward influence attempts that have little or nothing to do with firm strategy. Instead, the examples they mention have more to do with the manager's self-interest than with organizational interests. To a large degree this helps explain the unfortunate stereotypes we so often hear about from senior executives. To help managers avoid undermining their own effectiveness then, we have found it useful to differentiate legitimate championing from three other, more opportunistic forms of upward influence.

The Malcontent

Middle managers sometimes use upward influence as a way to vent frustrations with their position or status in the firm. This may be an expression of anger associated with carrying out the downsizing process. It may be an objection to the feasibility of some other kind of plan. It may be resentment over diminished career prospects. Whatever the subject matter, these communications are born of negative emotions and often framed as put-downs or criticisms of the organization and its leadership.

Why would a manager broadcast negativity upward toward superiors? Tom Brown, a management consultant in Louisville, Kentucky, gives three reasons for what he calls the "gray-cloud" manager's behavior.[5] First, he may feel betrayed if he has a feeling of being saddled with unrealistic expectations in the face of inadequate resources. Whether true or not, such circumstances make one feel abandoned and vulnerable to hostile forces. Second, many managerial malcontents have not had a developmental experience in years. As a result they feel underskilled and self-consciously out-of-date. Lack of confidence triggers self-degradation and an unrealistic denial of what they can reasonably accomplish. Third, some of these managers are close to retirement. Coupled with feelings of betrayal and lack of confidence, the sense of their own imminent departure leads to the desire to simply "coast." As one manager pleaded to his company's controller, "Just leave things alone for a couple more years, and then I'll be out of here."[6]

In another organization, we had firsthand experience with a gray-cloud manager. In fact, Joe, who is vice president of manufacturing for a Texas manufacturer, sometimes rains so hard he might more aptly be characterized as a Texas-sized "gully-washer." Joe is no Texan, however. In his late fifties, Joe learned manufacturing in Erie, Pennsylvania, and his basic philosophy is "to do as much as possible with as little as possible." Although he was hired for his penny-pinching mentality, the company president discovered over a period of three or four years that part of Joe's approach was to change as little as possible. Thus, when the chief engineer got encouragement from the president's office for a proposal to automate one of the production lines, Joe's penchant for carping behavior showed itself immediately.

> They don't listen to me. Unless you're one of the chosen few—the golden boys—your opinion just isn't worth much. Whenever I've suggested how things were done at [my previous company] or give them some input, I get ignored. I can see him [the boss] turning off. He says he hired me for my input, but why doesn't he listen?

Not surprisingly, when we asked the president about championing behavior among his subordinates, his response apparently reflected experience with Joe: "Some people are just never happy, and you can't respond to all their complaints."

Whatever the cause of the manager's discontent, perceived lack of top management support is used as an excuse for continued negativism. Left unchecked, the cycle continues, and the manager may become totally marginalized because top management comes to see his attempts at upward influence as little more than naysaying. The effect of this negative dynamic is to discourage even legitimate interactions. In these cases, the middle manager's potential for positive strategic influence disappears, and this can limit the firm's innovative capacity.

The Empire Builder

A second way middle managers misuse upward influence is to champion proposals that do little else than feather their own nests. Ambitious middle managers are quick to learn the skills of effective upward influence and often present well-reasoned justifications for their proposals. When the motivation is individual or even departmental payoff rather than organizational benefits, however, suspicion grows over time, and decreasing levels of trust within the organization cause relationships to weaken.

Consider, for example, how a middle manager we interviewed described one of her peers. "Bob has a lot of good ideas, and he really knows how to get things done. But you have to watch his motives. Whenever he asks for something, watch out! More times than not he has a hidden agenda."

Empire builders are generally more successful at upward influence than are malcontents. They use good arguments and offer "solutions" rather than complaints. After awhile, however, it usually becomes clear that they define "winning" in terms that are too narrow to be truly strategic. When adopted, their proposals yield more to the individual manager or her allies than they benefit the organization, and frequently there is a cost to some other subunit or individual. The manager's success therefore undermines not only her relationships with superiors but also with peers. Subordinates, on the other hand, can become quite loyal to an empire builder because they see her as a champion of their agenda. When empire building is prevalent, middle managers across the organization become increasingly suspicious of one another's motives and turf battles become the norm.

J. J. LaFranco has worked in the administrative branch of the finance department of a major northeastern aerospace company for just over twenty years. He has been head of the department for nearly a decade and is widely recognized for his administrative competence. With few exceptions, his subordinates hold him in high regard, and most refer to him affectionately as "J. J." A discussion with the firm's financial vice president, J. J.'s boss, however, made it clear that someone in the VP's unit was not always seen as a team player. Though he never mentioned J. J. by name, it became obvious how his comments applied.

I have to be careful about taking advice. Some of my subordinates have been here longer than I have, and they always make such a good argument. One in particular probably knows more than anyone about how the system works. But, I am trying to run my organization like a team. When I get the group together [the vice president's direct-reports included the controller as well as the directors of treasury, information systems, and administration] to discuss resource decisions, there is always tension. I attribute it to a lack of trust. It's as though they see the decision as a zero-sum game with winners and losers. Its frustrating. Bob [the division president] says we want everyone thinking like an entrepreneur. Well, some of my people think like entrepreneurs, but the business they're building isn't [the division's]. They're more concerned with who gets to manage which resources than with how the resources can be managed best.

Empire builders are thus more likely to be a source of corporate rigidity than a source of innovation and strategic initiative. Real championing means proposing alternatives that serve the needs of the organization. Initiatives that defend or advance personal or subunit self-interest can be masked (even unconsciously) as strategic responses. This leads many top managers to be understandably wary of enthusiastic middle managers bearing proposals.

Perhaps even more perniciously, empire building sets up a norm of competition among peers. Narrow perspectives make collaboration and teamwork more difficult and drive out the mindset needed to become an effective champion of strategic change.

The Reactive Manager

Whereas malcontents and empire builders are focused more on their own interests than on those of the organization, the reactive manager is genuinely interested in advancing the organization's objectives. Due to either a lack of experience or an inadequate perspective, however, these managers seem to react to every suggestion that comes their way. They become excited by their immediate surroundings and tend to be focused on whatever it is they have most recently been told.

David is director of national sales in the refrigeration division of a leading appliance manufacturer. His reputation as a salesman is unexcelled within the company, and distributors see him as the chief representative of the customers' interests. In many ways, he is the ultimate boundary-spanner and devotes much of his time conveying market feedback to other functions. Invariably, the market input is accompanied by a proposed change in the product design, service policy, promotional approach, and so on. Both his peers and his superior listen to what he says, but his ideas for dealing with a situation are heavily discounted. David's superior, the vice president of marketing, describes the situation this way.

> David has a tendency to overreact. In one of our weekly meetings, he conveyed a suggestion by a large distributor that we match [an upscale competitor's] warranty program. He'd asked for time on the agenda, and I had given it to him. But, he spent twenty minutes presenting a new warranty policy that was clearly out of the ballpark. Our product is in the middle of the market, and it was obvious to everyone in the room that David's argument was in left field. The distributor had really bent his ear, and at one point, it became clear where his argument was coming from. I know that his heart was in the right place, but it was another case of David being overly influenced by the last person he talked to.

Not surprisingly, reactives tend to be ineffective at influencing their superiors. First, they lack persistence and consistency. They quickly move from one issue to the next. Second, more emotional than analytical, they rarely do the homework necessary for effective championing. Many of their suggestions are off the cuff, and don't fit the company's priorities or capabilities.

Linked with an effective middle management champion, reactive managers can play a supporting role in the organization's innovative process. They can also be exploited by a savvy empire builder. More times than not, however, their proposals are shunned by peers and superiors alike. Consider David's boss's evaluation of his subordinate: "Dave is a very likable person, but I find myself avoiding contact with him. He's always got some harebrained idea that's going noplace. Sometimes he's interesting and I feel bad, but I really can't afford the time."

Each of the forms of upward influence presented above hampers the firm's dynamic renewal process. Both the malcontent and the reactive manager lose the confidence of upper management; the empire builder creates unnecessary conflict and distrust in the organization. We suspect readers are more likely to have seen these managers in their personal experience than they are to have had experience with the likes of a true middle management champion like Tom West. To help managers avoid slipping into a dysfunctional pattern, the list below highlights the characteristics of each type.

Counterproductive Upward Influence Characteristics

1. The Malcontent
   Criticizes top management frequently and without support
   Objects irrationally to management's plans
   Feels betrayed by top management
   Engages in self-degradation
2. The Empire Builder
   Conceals self-interest with rational arguments
   Is quick to offer solutions that benefit self
   Is extremely competent at manipulating "the system"
   Is mistrusted by peers and superiors for having hidden
      agendas
3. The Reactive Manager
   Hopes to serve organizational objectives
   Is easily influenced by recent experiences
   Lacks persistence, moving from one issue to the next
   Is ignored by peers and superiors

Restructuring as a Threat to Innovation

The case of Tom West demonstrates that middle management championing is not a new activity. Historically, however, championing has not been among middle management's primary activities. Many middle managers have never championed a strategic proposal. Yet business conditions continue to change, and as organizations struggle to adapt, there is an even greater need for the innovation created through championing. Hence middle managers' potential strategic influence in organizations is on the rise.

The realization of this potential, however, has too often been stunted by the restructuring effort itself. There are several reasons for this, one or more of which may be operating in a particular case. First, the climate of fear and uncertainty created by downsizing is not conducive to experimentation and risk taking. Second, the diminution of trust that accompanies round after round of unexpected and unexplained resource reductions provides little incentive to "go the extra yard," however necessary the downsizing may be. Third, surviving middle managers may be so overburdened with operational responsibilities that there is no longer leeway to do anything progressive. As one manager told us, "we're all just hanging on—trying to keep our heads above water."

Finally, negative behavior patterns are another barrier to realizing middle management's potential role in innovation. Divergent initiatives are naturally antagonistic to the status quo. Therefore, recognizing the difference between the malcontent, empire builder, and reactive manager as opposed to the true champion becomes a matter of understanding the manager's motivation. Believing that middle managers are the enemy creates a lens through which middle managers are much more likely to be seen as malcontents or empire builders. This can lead to rejection of sincere initiatives, thereby reinforcing the cycle of fear and mistrust between layers of management.

Sadly then, a movement that is premised on the need for dramatic organizational change has served to inhibit innovation in many organizations. A "quick fix" mentality in restructuring tends to dismantle organizational arrangements without a clear understanding of what is supposed to replace them. In our view, effective organizational redesign begins with a more enlightened understanding of how to reorient and redirect the work of middle management. We discuss this topic in Chapter Nine.

Summary

Middle management championing is fundamental to an organization's innovative process. Because it is confused with managerial discontent, empire building, and reactive management, this important form of upward influence is often under-recognized and unrewarded by top-level and even middle-level managers. Yet research has chronicled middle managers who act as catalysts for initiatives that move organizations in new and timely directions. As the case of Tom West shows, discrete and visible events such as championing a proposal to an executive committee really are the result of continuous activity in the other three roles.

Chapter Six

Synthesizing
Advancing Shared
Strategic Understanding

If championing represents the culmination of a process that increases innovation and expands the firm's repertoire of strategic capabilities, synthesizing represents the genesis of that process. Synthesizing the strategic significance of emergent events and information is something managers do all the time, naturally, as part of their day-to-day activities, sharing ideas, having conversations, reporting results to superiors, and so on. It provides the foundation for middle managers to effectively perform their other strategic roles.

Noting that synthesizing occurs naturally or automatically, however, in no way suggests that all managers perform this role equally well, or even adequately. It is an inherently subjective process that involves both intellectual and interpersonal skills. Intellectually, managers develop and constantly revise their own understanding of the strategic situation. Interpersonally, they influence the shared understanding of strategy within the organization through interactions with subordinates, peers, and top managers. *Synthesizing is a subjective process by which middle managers inject strategic meaning into operating and strategic information and communicate their interpretations to others.*

How managers come to understand the strategic situation and how they influence others' perceptions has a profound effect on the overall understanding of strategy that develops within the organization. In this chapter we take an explicit look at this fundamental yet somewhat subliminal role. In our experience, conscious attempts to improve one's synthesizing skills can greatly increase an individual's strategic value within a firm.

Elements of the Strategic Knowledge Base

Middle managers link the firm's strategic and operating domains, and as a result they are bombarded by streams of diverse data coming from both inside and outside the organization. By interpreting this diverse set of information and sharing it with others, including top managers, middle managers integrate new data with existing strategic thinking to help build the organization's strategic knowledge base.

The list that follows illustrates the elements that make up a firm's strategic knowledge base. Each of the types of information represents a piece of the strategic puzzle, and no one piece tells the entire story. Although top and operating-level managers are likely to be exposed to some of these elements, and indeed may develop in-depth knowledge about them, middle managers, particularly those in boundary-spanning positions, are the managers most likely to encounter the broadest range of these elements. As a result, they are often in the best position to help the organization integrate this diverse data— to put the pieces of the puzzle together.

Elements of the Strategic Knowledge Base

- *Existing Strategic Mindset.* Middle management's access to top management provides them with an in-depth understanding of the firm's current strategic logic. This understanding allows middle managers to comprehend the strategic significance of new information and thus influence the evolution of strategic thinking within the firm.
- *Customer Information.* The complexity and evolving nature of customer needs necessitates continuous learning within the organization. Research suggests that most new product innovations come from customers rather than the R&D lab.[1]
- *Competitor Information.* A knowledge of competitor strategies and aspirations is crucial in predicting the evolution of competition within an industry. Organizations learn not only new technologies and product innovations from competitors but also new operating processes and practices.
- *Network Information.* Organizational strategy can also be informed by firms in related and supporting industries.[2] To an extent, this type of learning is easier, as it does not involve

direct competition. Middle managers from different firms who belong to the same professional association, for example, may exchange information without threatening their firm's competitive advantage.

- *Process Knowledge and Information.* Middle management's hands-on involvement in operations provides them with an in-depth knowledge of operating processes and informs them of new developments and enhancements to existing capabilities as they emerge. Process knowledge is important at the work group, intrafunctional, and interfunctional levels, and middle managers who transcend these boundaries are needed to interpret process issues within a strategic context.
- *Technical Knowledge and Information.* Middle management's involvement in operations gives them a working knowledge of relevant technologies. This technical literacy allows middle managers to assess emerging technology issues within a strategic framework.

Many companies, for example, have struggled with the question of how to build an information system that creates competitive advantage. In one case, we studied a large stationery company where the general manager had come to see customer service as the top item on the strategic agenda. His interest in information technology had been stimulated by a computer vendor's presentation on electronic data interchange (EDI), a system that would give customers direct access to the company's data base. A study was initiated. Working with consultants, data processing and customer service managers began to define the requirements for the new technology. In the process, it became apparent that implementation demanded more detailed reporting and much higher accuracy than the manager of customer service believed was either feasible or desirable. In a sharply worded memo, the customer service manager informed the division's general manager that EDI was "totally unnecessary and inappropriate."

Fortunately, the director of marketing, who had not been involved in the project, received a copy of the testy memorandum. After discussing it with the frustrated general manager, he called a meeting that involved a consultant, a computer vendor representative, and the manager of customer service. In the meeting, the marketing director used his knowledge of what one of the firm's distributors was doing in order to show the customer service manager that EDI had come to the stationery industry and was "here to stay." The director made arrangements for the customer service manager to visit the distributor and see the system in action. After the visit, the supervisor of customer service wrote another memo to the general manager. This one asserted that although it would be costly and time consuming, implementation of EDI was a "crucial strategic investment that this company must now undertake."

The example illustrates again the importance of middle management's unique position. The senior manager believed that EDI fit the strategy, but he was in a poor position to argue with the operating-level manager who knew more about the details. It was a middle manager who was able to appreciate both the strategic implications of EDI and the practical problems of implementation. Admittedly, this manager knew less about the technical details than did operating manager, but he was able to frame the issue in a way that was convincing to all involved. In short, the manager was able to integrate EDI into the organization's shared understanding of strategy.

This example is by no means unique. If you think of an organization and its environment as a vast social network consisting of top- and operating-level managers, customers, suppliers, consultants, competitors, and so on, middle managers have the potential to encounter more different types of these contacts than anyone else in the network.[3] This is a normal result of the way job responsibilities are distributed: top managers have responsibility for strategy, operating managers for operations, and middle managers have responsibility for bringing the two together.

Organizational Learning

Noting the centrality of middle managers is not meant to suggest that they are the source of all organizational knowledge. Often they are simply in the best position to combine diverse bits of information into an overall strategic picture. The degree to which this positioning is exploited to the benefit of the organization, however, depends on how well the organization learns.

Figure 6.1 shows how an individual manager's synthesis or interpretation of events fits into the larger context of organiza-

**Figure 6.1. The Role of Core Values and Individual
Synthesizing in Organizational Learning.**

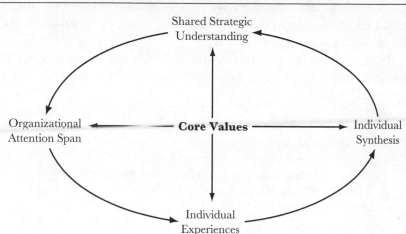

tional learning. At the heart of any organizational knowledge base
are a set of core values shared by organization members. In general, values represent the strongest filter on a person's perceptual
lens, affecting how she sees the world as an individual or as a member of an organization. Values define what we see as important,
what we pay attention to, what we believe is right and wrong or true
and false. The figure shows how core values shape the experiences
and interpretations of individuals and influence what the organization pays attention to, and how members of the organization
come to a common understanding of the strategic situation.

The centrality of core values to organizational learning in general, and middle management synthesizing in particular, is perhaps
best illustrated by a comparative example. Imagine two medium-
size machine shops. Both firms supply machined components to
manufacturers producing various types of consumer products. In
fact, the firms are almost identical *except* in terms of their dominant
core values.

The first firm is best characterized as autocratic. Managers
know they have limited influence on what the firm does and have
learned over time that their chief responsibilities are to act as expe-
diters and problem solvers. They are paid to see that things get
done, not to question what needs to be done.

Thinking about business-level issues is much less restricted in the second firm. The words *and actions* of the firm's president and owner convey that managers are expected to add value by "influencing the direction of the firm—figuring out how to survive in an increasingly competitive industry."

Now suppose the purchasing manager of each firm receives the following letter from a large customer.

> Dear Sir or Madam:
>
> In an effort to better control the quality of our company's products we have modified our policies regarding subcontractors. Beginning January 1, we are requiring all subcontractors to evaluate and "qualify" all vendors who supply raw material for the components we buy.
>
> In this regard, we ask that your company site-visit and document the quality control procedures of relevant firms. Thank you for your timely attention to this matter. I think you'll agree that ensuring quality is to our mutual benefit.
>
> Sincerely,
> Colin Irving
> Purchasing Director
> XYZ Corporation

In the first firm, the manager is likely to consider the request a nuisance and perhaps a waste of time. She is unlikely to recognize the potential strategic significance of the request. More likely, the manager will simply seek top management direction.

In the second firm, however, the manager may begin to consider the broader significance of the request. He may, for example, have become aware of emerging international quality standards and understand that meeting such standards is increasingly important within the industry. Combining this knowledge with his understanding of the firm's competitive circumstance, the manager may begin to describe to others how adopting quality standards could constitute a strategic advantage for the firm. In this case, a seemingly straightforward customer request has become the basis for investigation and discussion within the organization and ultimately might result in the firm gaining new competitive capabilities.

In essence, the lesson is that core values instilled by top management determine the strategic value of middle managers as synthesizers of information, and this in turn determines the degree of shared learning that occurs within the organization. Middle managers have the potential to advance strategic understanding in the firm by making connections among a wide variety of information elements and constituencies. The extent to which this potential is realized, however, relies heavily on the leadership reflected in the firm's system of core values.

How Categories Influence Strategic Thinking

Categorization is one of the tangible results of the interpretation process and a powerful way middle managers influence strategic thinking in others. Perhaps as a result of our evolutionary conditioning, the human mind insists on classifying events in a way that indicates the needed response. ("Is this beast approaching in the dark a saber-toothed tiger or my lovely mate?") Thus, a positive or negative slant becomes evident in the use of words like *problem, surprise, warning,* and so on.

Categories are useful in organizations because names or labels carry meaning that is easily transferable among members. Categorization is a form of mental shorthand that aids communication. Categories are rarely neutral. Labels and names have important effects on how information is interpreted. In short, the use of categories shapes shared strategic understanding.[4]

As middle managers interpret information in light of firm strategy, the two generic categories that surface most often are opportunity and threat. Use of these labels affects the evolving interpretation of an issue within the organization and thereby influences subsequent decision making. Researchers who have presented decision makers with identical scenarios, differing only with respect to whether they are represented as a threat or opportunity, have identified systematic differences in the kind of decision that is made and in the process used to reach the decision.

In the summer of 1984, one of the authors was conducting research interviews at the headquarters of IBM. The purpose was to assess how computers were being used by managers and professionals, but conversations frequently turned to the computer industry and how changes brought on by the PC would affect the company. The product planning group was participating in the study, and managers in this department had produced an enormous number of graphs and charts, all projecting rapid growth in microcomputer software and much slower growth in hardware. After several conversations, it became apparent that middle managers within IBM saw this trend as an opportunity. The charts even used titles like "software market opportunities."

At the time, this seemed odd to those of us on the research team because the company had already given up control over development of the PC's operating system to Microsoft. Many industry observers believed this would give Bill Gates's young company a huge competitive advantage. In hindsight, it is apparent that IBM's culture refused to accept the idea that a newly formed and still tiny software company could pose a significant threat to "Big Blue." Not seeing the growth in software as a threat to their industry dominance, IBM made only modest investments in software development within the company, relying instead on an alliance with Microsoft to address the issue. By the late 1980s the window of time for a viable strategic response had closed, and IBM was essentially shut out of the PC software market.

Table 6.1 summarizes the research concerning the effects of category labeling on strategic decision making. On the whole it demonstrates that how an issue is labeled has an important effect on how an organization responds. When an issue is described as an opportunity, it is likely to be seen as bringing something positive into the situation, something the organization can control and that will create a gain. An opportunity for the most part already fits the organization's strategy, so the changes needed inside the company are seen to be fairly incremental. Much of the organization's effort will focus not on organizational change but on leveraging their control over external events.

The same issue framed as a threat, however, would be seen negatively, as something relatively uncontrollable. The established strategy would be perceived as ill suited, and managers would likely respond with large-scale changes inside the company. By their labeling of events and trends as threats or opportunities, therefore, middle managers can play an important role in determining how an issue is understood within the organization and how top management is likely to respond.

Table 6.1. How Categories Influence Strategic Decision Making.

Category Label	Implications for the Decision Process	Implications for the Nature of the Decision
Opportunity (generally understood as controllable and as a potential gain)	Tends to increase the number of alternatives considered and broaden participation in strategic decision making	Tends to evoke decisions involving incremental or small-scale changes targeted at the external environment
Threat (generally understood as uncontrollable and as a potential loss)	Tends to contrain the number of alternatives considered and reduce participation in strategic decision making. Decisions and changes tend to follow a top-down pattern.	Tends to evoke large-scale responses involving significant change. Decisions are more likely to focus on internal realignments.

Data adapted from Jane E. Dutton and Susan E. Jackson, "Categorizing Strategic Issues: Links to Organization Action," *Academy of Management Review*, 1987, *12*, 76–90.

More broadly, there are an almost infinite number of other ways middle managers can frame strategic issues. They can frame an event as related to a particular function—for example, as a human resource issue, a technology issue, as a quality issue, and so on—or they can frame it as an issue affecting the whole business. They can frame it is as more or less urgent. They can emphasize certain facets of the issue over others. In describing an issue, middle managers can even incorporate a proposed solution. Each of these dimensions will influence how others see the issue, and this in turn will affect related decisions.[5]

Selling Our Impressions to Others

The way an issue is framed affects how much attention an idea gets. As we have seen, threats get more attention than opportunities. Similarly, ideas that are seen as urgent, new, or different are more likely to be heard by top managers. The number of people involved also affects how much attention an issue receives. A coalition of people, such as a cross-functional group of middle managers, is much more likely to be heard than a single individual. Finally, top management is not likely to pay attention when an issue is ambiguous or poorly argued. Middle managers who are successful at getting the attention of others know how to make a clear, concise case for their ideas, using persuasive evidence and sound logic.[6]

Les was the national manager of franchise sales for a major fast-food restaurant chain. He had come into the restaurant industry after ten years' experience as a branch sales manager for Xerox, a company that many believe provides the best sales training in the world. Les's compensation was based in part on his ability to recruit new licensees for the burger chain, and after just two years in his position, he had been responsible for licenses that resulted in the construction of more than two hundred new restaurants. His success gave him immense credibility with senior management.

The issue that arose, however, was that fifty-two of the new units had been licensed to just one new franchisee. The franchisee was a restaurant operator in the Midwest with two other restaurant chains, in addition to the new hamburger stores. Although the franchisee's size and expertise allowed the company to grow quickly, the downside was that a large licensee could wield considerable clout. In this case, a conflict arose between the corporate operations group and the franchisee about how to change the menu to suit regional tastes. Corporate operations argued that menu changes under-mined national standards and therefore threatened a key aspect of the chain's competitive strategy. Because they were experienced restaurateurs, management in the franchisee asserted they were going ahead with the changes, and if necessary, they would "take down the sign" in order to accomplish this, meaning they would cancel their franchise.

Not surprisingly, Les argued forcefully within the company on the side of franchisee. He successfully framed the issue as a necessary adaptation of national standards to suit regional tastes. This was an emerging strategy being pursued by competitors, he argued, and cor-porate operations were "sticking their heads in the sand" if they thought they could preserve a uniform national standard. In a crucial presentation to the executive committee, Les showed how rival chains had permitted regional differences and increased market share as a result. The operations group had no way to counter this argument, relying instead on the traditional logic of standardization. In comparison to the case Les was making, the operations group's arguments seemed dated.

Les succeeded in reshaping the organization's understanding of strategy, and in the short term, this preserved the relationship with the large franchisee. In addition, however, the concessions opened a floodgate of demands for menu changes from other, smaller licensees across the country. Coping with these put enormous strains on corporate policy and franchisee relations, not to mention the pressure it put on operations to change kitchen equipment design and employee training procedures. Today, in a saturated and highly competitive fast food market, the menu and operational differences across the chain have become a serious hurdle to maintaining quality and cost standards.

The reality is that managers differ considerably in their ability to frame an issue, to build a coalition, and to make a coherent argument. Too often it seems that the manager who is good at getting top management attention, like Les, is trying to feather his own nest rather than serve the interests of the organization. Indeed, it is this ability of self-interested issue sellers to manipulate the organization's strategic understanding and thereby shape the strategic agenda that causes top managers to be suspicious of middle management input.

Manipulation or Leadership: Two Views of the Synthesizing Role

So how should we view middle management's issue selling in the synthesizing role? Is it manipulation or leadership? Top management's fear is that managers will select and bias information to promote their own interests. Self-interest in itself is not necessarily bad, however. What is critical is the extent to which the middle manager's interests and those of the organization overlap. Certainly, the burger chain benefited from Les's sales efforts, which were highly motivated by his self-interest. As long as personal goals are congruent with organizational goals, self-interested synthesizing is likely to serve the organization.

Unfortunately, in many cases it may be difficult to know, even for the issue seller herself, whether the argument is congruent with organizational interests. A better solution to the problem of self-interest, then, is to promote a diversity of viewpoints in the process of building shared strategic understanding. Problems arise when only one voice is heard. Whether the dominant voice is that of a middle- or top-level manager, *the potential for losing sight of the organization's interests increases in inverse relationship to the number of perspectives being shared.* In fact, as we have seen in the case of championing, one of the chief advantages of increasing middle management involvement is to increase the breadth of alternative perspectives.

Common sense and research on decision making supports this. Studies of management groups seeking a consensus on strategy show that higher-quality decisions result from a process that includes conflict. That is, a willingness to tolerate and even seek out diverse viewpoints brings more information to light and creates a more accurate appraisal of the strategic circumstances.[7] Just as Les's dominance of the argument within the restaurant chain led to a low-quality decision, a top manager's dominance of an organization's understanding of strategy can lead to low-quality decisions. The most famous example of this is Irving Janis's description of "groupthink" and the decision to invade Cuba in 1961. Self-censoring on the part of cabinet members out of deference to the new president kept crucial information from being brought to the decision.[8]

The admonition we would make is that top managers, rather than coping with the problem of self-interested issue selling by listening *less* to middle managers, should seek input and listen to the perspectives of *more* middle managers. The value of this recommendation, of course, depends on a degree of balance among middle management synthesizers. Instead of being dominated by the few, such as Les, who are talented issue sellers, organizations will benefit from more effective synthesizing by many middle managers.

A Framework for Effective Influence

There are many ingredients to becoming an influential issue seller. Good communication skills are paramount, for example; however, this is not a book on effective communication. Instead, Table 6.2 summarizes the major considerations in issue selling, emphasizing in particular the importance of categorization and framing to the synthesizing process. There will be many cases when a middle manager is synthesizing without a specific agenda. The guidelines here

Table 6.2. Framework for Effective Influence.

Goal	Novelty	Urgency	Category	Relevance
Add issue to the strategic agenda	New	Urgent		
Motivate significant change in organization structure or process	New	Urgent	Threat	
Motivate significant change in strategy	New	Urgent	Threat	Businesswide

are intended for use on those occasions when synthesizing is purposeful, that is, when middle management's intention is to influence organizational action in some specific way.

The first question to ask in issue selling is, What is the goal? Naturally, a middle manager's motivation may emphasize the three goals shown in Table 6.2 to a greater or lesser extent or combine them in some way. The table suggests that the more one of the goals is present in the manager's intention, the more important each of the descriptors is to the issue-selling process. The inverse is also true, and it is possible to generate an overreaction on the part of top management. If one simply wants to initiate a dialogue within the organization about an issue, it is not necessary to represent the issue as a major threat or to suggest it has businesswide implications. Instead, framing it as novel and relatively urgent will probably get it on the table.

Jim, for example, was the director of information management for a medium-size health maintenance organization (HMO) that participated in one of our studies. Returning from a "New Health Care Technologies" conference, he began to create doubt about the future prospects of his organization. Among other managers and staff, he talked cynically about the firm's physician outcomes monitoring system, which was intended to help ensure appropriate utilization of health care services. Utilization management is crucial in an HMO's effort to strike a balance between high-quality and low-cost care. The technology had been developing rapidly, and Jim repeatedly asserted to his colleagues, "We're not even in the ballpark." More important, in a memo to his boss about the conference, Jim created a sense of crisis. "I'm not sure what the impact of the new systems will be, but our competitors already have it up and running. I don't understand the stuff myself, and I'm sure nobody else around here does!"

For top management, Jim's reaction to the conference spoke volumes. Jim's boss had asked him to attend the conference in order to stay on top of developments in the field. But Jim's reaction created a sense of urgency and threat to the entire business. Change was coming and the organization seemed ill-prepared to cope with it. In response to the "crisis," top management hired a consulting firm whose recommendations included an overall restructuring of the information systems organization, significant shifting of responsibilities, and companywide training. Along the way, Jim lost influence and authority and eventually left the firm. In our conversation with the CEO, he admitted that Jim's approach to the problem was "probably overkill. We could have accomplished the same thing with far fewer resources and much less turmoil."

Jim's experience in this case illustrates the tight connection between middle management behavior and top management action. Jim's panic, generated by his own lack of understanding and doubts about the company's systems, caused top management to perceive the situation as urgent and threatening. They then took control of the situation, imposing an admittedly draconian solution. Jim had oversold the issue.

A final point to remember is that a group can sell any issue of significance more easily than can a single individual. If you are the only one who thinks its important, it probably isn't. Typically, motivating strategic change represents the "hardest sell," so coalitions may need to be broadest for this purpose; however, significant organizational changes, even if they do not represent a major change in strategy, may still affect a large number of people, many of whom represent potential opposition. To be an effective issue seller, one needs many of the political skills (discussed in Chapter Five) used to build support for a particular proposal. In fact, it is when an issue begins to evolve into a solution that coalition building becomes important.

This point illustrates again the overlap among the four roles, and in particular the way that synthesizing strategic information frequently is a precursor to championing a strategic alternative.

Synthesizing, and especially issue selling, is an essential aspect of championing.

Summary

In the synthesizing role, middle managers are participating in a wider, organizational interpretation process in which everyone plays a role, and clearly, top and operating-level managers have important influence. The unique set of interactions afforded middle managers, however, gives them the opportunity to synthesize meaning from an exceptionally wide range of inputs. Whether an individual's interpretation helps the organization learn depends significantly on the extent to which organization members share a set of core values. Successful organizational learning also depends on management's ability to frame ideas and sell issues that positively effect the organization's shared understanding of its strategic circumstances. The list below summarizes the hallmarks of an effective synthesizer.

Hallmarks of Effective Synthesizing

- Proactive Learning

   Comprehends and articulates the strategic mindset
   Internalizes and externally tests core values
   Imports and interprets strategic information

- Deliberate Communicating

   Actively frames issues in accord with strategic significance
   Selectively sells issues that warrant response
   Adjusts "sales approach" to achieve desired goals

Chapter Seven

Facilitating
Nurturing Adaptability and
Setting the Stage for Renewal

We saw how middle managers in the synthesizing role help to build the knowledge base that underlies organizational capability. One can think of synthesizing therefore as the mental or cognitive side of organizational learning. Learning also has an experiential element, however. More specifically, unless organization members have opportunities to engage in behaviors that stretch beyond the demands of existing routines, no significant new knowledge is likely to be accumulated. Expecting learning to occur without novel or "out of the box" experiences would be like expecting science to make progress without ever conducting experiments.

In the strategic role we call *facilitating*, middle managers create laboratory-like conditions within their subunit. Information is freely shared; normal rules of the operating environment are suspended or held constant; people try new things (experimental trials); and everyday resource constraints are temporarily suspended. By sheltering nonroutine activity, managers produce conditions where the experiences critical to organizational learning can occur. Formally, we define the facilitating role as *the nurturing and development of experimental programs and organizational arrangements that increase organizational flexibility, encourage organizational learning, and expand the firm's repertoire of potential strategic responses.*

The Cycle of Organizational Change

Why is it that so many large organizations must come to the point of crisis before they recognize the need for change? Following years of consistent growth, many companies seem to face a similar scenario. First, there is a gradual deterioration in financial performance. Rumors are heard among insiders that the company is losing its way. Despite early warnings, management stays with the "historically proven" strategy. Then the profit picture worsens, until the corporation faces a cash crisis or falls into the hands of a corporate raider. At the point of breakdown, significant change is initiated, and the impetus often comes from board members who are not senior managers.

This pattern—periods of stability punctuated by drastic upheaval—is familiar to anyone who has managed or observed business organizations. The costs of slow response in both human and financial terms are enormous, frequently threatening the firm's survival. Reasons for the unfortunate pattern lie in the environment, where jolts like deregulation, entry of foreign competition, and so on, create new rules that catch managers by surprise. But external change is only part of the explanation. The other factor is *organizational inertia.*[1]

Inertia is associated with the choice of a particular set of goals and strategies (Figure 7.1). Organizational commitment to a new strategy is likely to be tentative in the early stages of its life cycle. As time passes and the strategy proves successful, however, more and more organization members become convinced. Esteem for senior management who created the strategy increases. Success makes decision makers look even wiser in retrospect than they seemed in the beginning. Respect for top management and resolution of the strategy reach a zenith in the organization just about when financial and market payoffs begin to plateau. Coupled with the systems, structures, norms, and values necessary to institutionalize a strategy, commitment and devotion to an individual or group become inertial forces that create a "snowball effect." Potential alarms embodied in negative financial signals are filtered out by managers who are acutely aware of investments made to support the existing strategy. Other warnings are ignored or explained away as uncontrollable "market conditions." Ultimately, like the force that builds in the tectonic plates, stress accumulates to an intolerable level, and the organizational equilibrium is shaken to its core by an earthquake of change.[2]

To avoid the costs of crisis, and to survive and prosper in the long run, organizations need to foster a certain degree of disorder—disaffection with the status quo—as well as commitment and

Figure 7.1. Strategic Change and Inertia.

Stage in the Cycle of Strategy	Stress/Inertia Levels
Formation	Low/Low
Early implementation success	Moderate/Building momentum
Established, successful plan	Moderate/Full speed ahead
Environmental or financial signs of vulnerability	High/Snowball effect
Crisis	Breaking point

stability. Stability is needed in basic structures, relationships, and control systems. At the same time, an awareness of the vulnerabilities in even the most successful strategy is useful in balancing inertial forces. By the time warning signals get attention, environmental shifts may have already happened, and quick response requires an array of partly proven alternatives. Thus, in addition to healthy self-criticism, there is a need for ongoing experimentation and discovery, finding new ways of doing things. The learning accumulated from such informal trials may later provide the basis for more fundamental strategic redirection. In short, organizations need the flexibility that comes from experimentation both in order to cope with day-to-day surprises and to offset the forces of inertia.[3]

Middle Managers' Dilemma and the Adaptation Process

Major upheavals and radically new strategies are almost always led by new leadership at the top.[4] But in our work we've found that it is middle-level managers who orchestrate the adjustments necessary to facilitate incremental adaptation. Left unattended, inertia will perpetuate the status quo. Change does not occur without proactive managerial efforts, and by facilitating adaptability within their organizational units, middle managers play a crucial role in fighting the creeping inertia that occurs over the course of a strategy's life cycle.

This puts middle managers on the horns of a dilemma. On the one hand, facilitating calls for loosening the reins, encouraging informality and stimulating risk taking in others. On the other hand, because middle managers are the ones who implement strategy, they also create and administer the structures and systems that impose stability. Pulled in opposite directions, middle management's potential to facilitate change may go unrealized because there is often far more reinforcement for successful implementing than for facilitating.

One reason for this difficult state of affairs stems from the misperceptions of middle management work outlined in Chapter One. Another reason is that implementing is consistent with top management's strategy. Successful implementors are good soldiers. Facilitating, however, means behaving in ways that diverge from, and perhaps even undermine, top management's stated intention. By engaging subordinates in activities that don't contribute to formal goals, facilitators may look as though they are dragging their feet or squandering resources. Worse still, they may be seen as managerial mutineers.

The almost schizophrenic character of the two roles and the overwhelming tendency to reward good soldiers[5] make facilitating the most problematic of the four middle management roles. Yet without a little subversion, the organization becomes doomed to an inevitably obsolete course of action, incapable of creating innovation. As Joseph Schumpeter observed, innovation is the outcome of "creative destruction."[6] Effective organizational adaptation then, to some degree, rests on establishing better understanding and clearer expectations of this difficult aspect of middle management work among both middle and top-level managers.

The following section depicts how the facilitating role emerges as a management response that moves beyond and contravenes deliberate strategy.

Two Sides of the Facilitating Process

A middle manager participating in a recent course provided a good illustration of the facilitating role. Like most defense contractors, his company faces declining demand from the U.S. defense establishment. As a result, the firm has begun to pursue opportunities in the commercial sector, where its products are used in transportation, construction, and offshore oil drilling.

The organization's high-tech history in government work has produced an enviable degree of expertise in product engineering. But there has been little incentive to reduce costs, a process innovation the company now needs badly in order to compete with more efficient commercial rivals.

In the early 1990s, top management announced a program of high-involvement work teams for the manufacturing work force. The teams' mission was process improvement. Team-based management was seen by insiders as an exceptional step for a company known for its functional orientation and engineering discipline. Internally, the program was met with widespread skepticism and passive resistance.

Even though teams had been instituted only for production workers, a group of salaried employees was eager to form a team. They wanted to deal with a particularly stubborn set of production control problems. The middle manager in charge of the area was encouraging, and ultimately he facilitated creation of a group to streamline the scheduling process.

According to a human resource professional observing the team, good relationships within the group had been skillfully fostered by the manager for two or three years. His consistent team-building effort paid off when the young team produced several immediate successes. Less than a year after forming the team, however, the middle manager was offered a promotion outside the department.

Almost simultaneously, the company announced a reduction in staff, and team members—many of them managers themselves—feared that their group could easily become a target. But the level of information sharing among team members and the experiences they had shared as successful problem solvers led them to consider self-management—something totally new and foreign to the firm's hierarchical norms. The group had already experimented with self-management under the high-involvement leadership of their department head. As a result, when senior management approved and formally announced the formation of the company's first self-managed team, the team had already been functioning for several months.

This example illustrates the two facets of the facilitating role. First, notice that the middle manager's early nurturing and ultimately his sponsorship of self-management diverged from top management intention. Under some circumstances, self-management might be a natural extension of high-involvement work teams, but this evolution was, if anything, discouraged by a strongly hierarchical culture. As in many companies, "high involvement" meant "higher contribution" but not a challenge to the idea of hierarchy. Had the idea of self-management been explicitly proposed in the early going, it would have been rejected. There was no explicit violation of company policy here, but the manager was subtly subversive, sheltering behavior that fell outside organization norms. This is the subversive, "destructive" side of the role.

Second, the climate of openness and trust created by the middle manager led subordinates to experiment with new behaviors, learning to share responsibilities as a team before taking on the greater burden of self-management. The manager's umbrella permitted experimentation with a new set of norms. Risky behaviors, such as challenging a superior or confronting a personality conflict, emerged in an environment that encouraged exploration. It was up to the manager to control the initial chaos and simultaneously keep the daily work moving. This is the nurturing, "creative" side of the role.

In combination, the two facets of facilitating provide the kind of "give" organizations need. This is why in Chapter Four we compared facilitation to the flexible, accordion-like structure between the two parts of a reticulated passenger bus. The shape and composition of the accordion are like the "give" within the team. Informality, produced by the manager's style, is injected into the formal structure and gives it flex. This overcomes rigidities in the vehicle while at the same time ensuring that front and back move in the same direction.

The Subversive Middle Manager

Despite all the recent talk about empowerment, the behaviors associated with facilitating adaptability have long been seen by top management as subversive. In 1970, Joseph Bower described the resulting tension in a large chemical company whose middle management diverted resources and hid experimental programs from top management. In one case, plant managers discovered a new fertilizer formula, created a small production line, and even test-marketed the product, before taking a new venture proposal to top management.[7] Not surprisingly, our own more recent interviews[8] suggest that some top managers view this role cynically.

To be effective as a facilitator, middle managers need to maintain an "informed skepticism" about top management's plans. This means that while they understand and even respect the strategy, they resist becoming committed to it as the *only* means of success.[9] Sometimes that skepticism can be explicit, as when the manager goes public with subordinates. A middle manager in one of the consulting firms we studied, for example, described how he regularly corrected subordinates' perceptions about what the "real" situation was, versus what the CEO said it was. "I simply informed the group after the boss had gone that just because he says it's that way doesn't make it so."

An attitude like this often leads to foot-dragging on the action plan. Whether this is good or bad depends on the reasons for the reluctance and whether or not the resistance is complemented by an alternative initiative. In the worst case, managers merely resist because their own interests are threatened. Resistance due to closed-mindedness and defending turf are anathema to innovation.[10]

In our experience, however, middle managers are more likely to have the organization's interests at heart. They may see the official plan as overly ambitious or otherwise unrealistic. The plan may be infeasible, calling on capabilities the organization really does not possess. It may be premature, or it may ignore some other essential facet of market or technical reality. In these cases, strategic middle managers often take the plan in directions not intended by top management.

For example, at a large regional office supply firm we are familiar with, top management, encouraged by recent success, decided to expand the commercial side of the business into two neighboring states. Pat, the sales manager, was instructed to hire additional sales personnel to cover the new region. She was skeptical of the new plan, however. Having worked for a competing firm in the proposed new region, Pat understood subtle differences between the two markets and felt strongly that the firm's first step would need to include the establishment of a "retail presence." Since "retail had never been the firm's forte," however, top management had dismissed this approach.

As a response, Pat was slow to hire additional staff and, initially, hired fewer people than top management had specified in the plan. In the interim, she laid the groundwork for a retail business, investigating locations and conducting market research. Notably, she told the new sales reps of the firm's "retail" plans and instructed them to "use this as a major selling point." As inquiries about the retail business were received at headquarters, the firm was ready to respond.

Thus middle management skepticism can be a boon, but it is likely to be perceived as a challenge to top management authority. To make matters worse, accumulating excess resources and experimenting covertly are necessary to facilitating, and they are usually incompatible with honest reporting under organizational control systems. These two factors make it impossible to formalize the facilitating role.

Even though most middle managers have been "empowered to make decisions," the tacit understanding is that these decisions will be consistent with top management's existing priorities. When the power is used to balance, undermine, or even override these priorities, relationships with the top inevitably become tense, if not hostile. Favorable resolution of an outright conflict ultimately depends on the middle manager's ability to build a case, in the form of either a reason for skepticism or a championed proposal. In either case, informal links with peers, outsiders (especially customers), and subordinates are key to legitimizing the argument. In Pat's case, for example, once she was found out "the confrontation was awful." In the end, however, her efforts were vindicated by the firm's success in the new region.

The potential for interpersonal conflict is a particularly challenging aspect of the effective facilitator role. The manager in charge of leasing for a diversified financial services company, for example, described to us the "shouting matches" he had with his superior, the unit's president.

> He continued to push his idea for standardizing contracts among our leasing units. Those of us who know vendor relationships were certain that standardization was impractical and could cost us business. He would come into our meetings and basically direct my people to change their contracts, and when I flat contradicted him, he went into hyperdrive!

Surprisingly, the willingness to bear the brunt of top management hostility often generates enormous respect among superiors. No one wants a yes-man, and most senior managers value constructive criticism and tolerate a heated dialogue. Yet, too many middle managers are unwilling or unable to stand the strain of doing battle, and given the potential impediments summarized in the list below, this may not be surprising. As Gene Koprowski, a management psychologist at the University of Colorado once observed, "most failure in management occurs not for lack of knowledge, but for lack of courage."

Organizational Impediments to the Facilitating Role

- Sheltered resources contravene formal controls
- Reward for "making the plan"
- Perceived challenge to top management authority
- Risk of formal sanction
- Potential for heated conflict

The Nurturing Middle Manager

To nurture means to create an environment where people can grow, develop, and learn; this describes the facilitating role's creative side. The origins of innovation can almost always be traced to the seed of an idea planted by someone from outside (customer, supplier, consultant, and so on) into the mind of someone inside the organization, usually at the operating level. Much of the time the seed falls on dry land, as the organization member fails to recognize how the idea might fit the organization's need. If the individual has the time and inclination to find opportunity, however, and if other members of the organization around her—including her manager—are open to the possibility of change, the seed begins to grow. While the biological metaphor may seem a bit strained, it represents the latest thinking about how innovation occurs in complex organizations.[11]

Balancing the need for efficient implementation and the nurture of creative adaptation is an ongoing challenge. At a minimum, top management expects progress toward agreed-upon goals with a given amount of resources. Yet the middle manager is faced with the fact that no matter how well-conceived the strategy, it is impossible to anticipate everything, and at some point the accepted course of action is likely to come under strain. Some time and effort must be spent nourishing adaptability apart from, and sometimes in spite of, the intentions embedded in top management's strategy.

Left unchecked, inertia—the forces of stability—will drive adaptability out. Resolving the dilemma requires proactive middle management behavior. First, and most fundamentally, good facilitators recognize the need for and become adept at creating organizational slack. They afford individuals in their units the opportunity to be responsive: to build productive relationships, to attend professional meetings and training sessions, to connect with customers, and so forth. Without some slack in the system, unit members have little or no opportunity to look up from the pace of daily routines and are thus in no position to allow for change, much less to develop and experiment with new ideas.

Second, having created the potential for innovation, nurturing middle managers are astute at creating organizational climates that encourage interpersonal trust and broad-based, strategic perspectives. In such environments, subordinates feel free to question the status quo, challenge conventional wisdom, and try new things. The rich knowledge base in the group provides the information needed to judge where slack is needed versus where to stay the course. The level of interpersonal trust determines whether members cooperate with one another. If there is true collaboration, it leads both to more creative problem solving and to smoother execution. This is because team building produces maximum utilization of the information brought by each individual and a high level of individual motivation for carrying out the team's decision.[12]

There are five specific behaviors associated with facilitating adaptability:

- Encouraging informal discussion and information sharing
- Relaxing regulations to get new projects started
- Buying time for experimental programs
- Locating and providing resources for trial projects
- Providing a safe haven for experimental programs

Notice that the same set of underlying process skills needed in these behaviors are also needed in deliberate team-building interventions. For example, encouraging people to share information openly requires astute observation of interpersonal dynamics. In essence, effective facilitating rests on the manager's sensitivity to group processes, the ability to coach others, and the willingness to be confrontational.

Team building is seen by many managers as a discrete set of activities, frequently involving some type of intervention by an outside facilitator. The strategic need for the facilitating role, however, means that middle managers need to incorporate team building into their repertoire of basic managerial behaviors.

The Link to Championing

The facilitating role is a crucial prerequisite of effective championing. Effectively facilitated, an organizational unit becomes a laboratory where new ideas are tested without official sanction, and subordinates closest to technical and customer conditions become the sources of initiative. Results accumulate on a small scale, and when the timing is right, the middle manager begins to build a case. Ultimately, championing becomes a matter of finding the fit between the pressures to change and top management's willingness to listen. The openness and interpersonal trust created by the middle management facilitator produce valuable information for the middle manager as champion. This in turn leads to higher-quality decision making on the part of top management and more successful innovation by the firm.[13]

Thus, although the immediate impact of the facilitating role is usually limited to a particular unit, its association with championing means that these local effects become the genesis of more significant innovation. In the case of the defense contractor, a human resources manager commented: "The manager's help in transitioning the team to a form of self-management allowed each team member to effectively become better managers themselves . . . [who] . . . are currently taking an active role in exploring new ways to bring scheduling to a world-class level." The middle manager was a mentor, nurturing the growth and learning that became the foundation of the firm's new capability.

Summary

Facilitating adaptability is critical to the organization's ongoing adaptation process. Without an effective adjustment mechanism, firms are unable to overcome the inertia associated with established practices, and over time face the need for radical, crisis-driven change. Middle managers facilitate adaptation by creating innovative organizational arrangements and nurturing promising operating-level initiatives. In many ways, facilitating adaptability lays the groundwork for successful middle management championing.

Chapter Eight

Implementing
Inducing the Vision and Making It Real

Like facilitating, implementing is about managing change. Rather than acting autonomously, however, middle managers in the implementing role inject new strategic priorities into the organization that emanate from the top.[1] In contrast with the incremental character of facilitating, implementation is associated with large-scale, formal change. Implementing deliberate strategy involves intervening in the organization's existing operations, creating new systems and structures. In essence, it is about redeploying organizational capabilities.

Often considered the primary strategic role of middle managers, implementation is usually conceived of simply as controlling activity with respect to top management goals. This is not all wrong. But as strategy making accelerates to keep pace with changing conditions, middle managers intervene again and again, altering and realigning key operating activities. In a world of continuous change, therefore, the usual view of implementation conceals the fact that specifying objectives must often be left to middle managers, as top managers concern themselves with more durable aspects of direction, such as values, vision, or "strategic intent."[2] We define implementation as *a series of interventions designed to align organizational action with strategic intent.*

Too often, managers think choosing the right strategy is the hard part. In reality, as one top manager told us, "It's been rather easy for us to decide where we wanted to go. The hard part is to get the organization to act on the new priorities." This gulf between strategy and execution is the "implementation gap," and a recent survey of Fortune 500 top executives suggests it may be growing. Only 6 percent believed that middle managers comply completely with business-level objectives.[3] Before describing the implementation role in detail, therefore, it may be worthwhile to develop an appreciation for the depth of the problem.

A Problem of Translation

Banking has seen as much downsizing as any industry in the United States. Most of the reductions follow what economists would call "in-market consolidations," mergers between banks whose branches are spread in the same general geographic area. Even though two banks may seem quite similar to an outsider, they can be quite different inside. Mergers almost always involve a major reorientation for at least one of the partners. The acquirer's strategy and systems, if not its structure and culture, must be implanted in the new operations. Thus, the challenge for a merger is "to make it work," and typically, top managers can allow no more than a year to successfully implement the combination.

Anthony "Tony" Terraciano is the chief executive of First Fidelity, the country's twenty-fourth-largest bank. After leading his organization through more than a half-dozen consolidations, he describes the decision process in two phases.

> First, there is the question of the desirability of the merger. This is a matter of trading off the efficiencies gained from the combination versus the increase in geographic risk. Reaching a "go or no go" decision is essentially an analytical game, and we have become quite good at this part of the process. The part that we, and I suspect others, have underestimated is the execution phase. It is far easier to crunch the numbers than it is to actually achieve the efficiencies. Mergers that have failed in our industry and elsewhere usually go bust because someone underestimated the barriers to execution or did not execute effectively.

Mr. Terraciano's observation is not unique. We frequently hear senior executives complain that middle and operating managers fail to take the actions necessary to implement a strategic change.

For their part, operating-level employees often do not even understand what the firm's strategy is. First Fidelity's Terraciano describes an experience he had about halfway through a consolidation process with a newly established bank group.

> This bank had gotten into trouble because they weren't making money in the commercial lending business. Like a lot of banks, they were making concessions to the big companies in order to put assets on the balance sheet, but they weren't generating any income. I spent several days going around to various groups of loan officers in order to explain personally my vision of the new strategy. I made the statement: "We are going to shift our customer base out of the jumbo and into the midsize market, and we are no longer going to waive lending fees for any of our customers." One of the guys stood up and said, "I don't understand the strategy." This flustered me. I repeated my previous statement, and asked him, "What don't you understand about the strategy?" "I just don't understand," he said. Then, in a flash, it came to me: this guy understood the words, but he didn't get it—or couldn't get it—because it went against everything his bank had been doing for the last ten years. Nobody in the middle had bothered to translate the strategy in a way that made any sense to him. He needed an explanation of what they'd been doing wrong and why it hadn't worked.

Underlying this communication gap is the reality that top executives and operating-level personnel speak separate languages. Top executives think and talk about strategy abstractly using such concepts as competitive advantage, market share, switching costs, and the like. They are goal oriented, knowing the results they want but having less of an idea about exactly how to achieve them. Operating personnel, on the other hand, are action oriented, thinking in terms of specific programs and day-to-day activities. They are concerned with finding the best way to do a specific job rather than questioning whether the job needs to be done. This group, in other words, is means oriented.

Given these separate orientations, effective implementation requires middle managers who can lead the process of translating abstract strategies into priorities that can be understood at lower levels. First, however, the operating personnel must be convinced that there is a solid rationale behind the new strategy. Otherwise, new strategies are met with skepticism and seen as "another management program." What this means is that middle managers must learn to communicate in two separate languages.

In the case of First Fidelity, Mr. Terraciano needed a middle manager from the parent bank to work directly with the new group of lending officers. The first step was to engage them in a conversation about the lending philosophies of the two banks and why one had proved more successful in the market than another. Then, as part of an action-planning session, the manager solicited objectives, methods, and accountabilities from the group. The action plan created the basis for an ongoing dialogue, and at the end of six months, the result was a lending policy that synchronized with the parent.

How Are We Doing? Establishing the Need for Change

Key to effective implementation is assessing the magnitude of desired change and providing appropriate motivation. To do this, managers need to change performance norms in a way that highlights the deficiencies of the current systems, structures, and people. As long as feedback about current conditions remains positive, the organization has little motivation to change. Because proactive strategy is needed before financial or market indicators turn sour, however, finding measures that motivate change can become a problem. Creative middle managers search for new benchmarks, demonstrating how performance standards previously considered acceptable are inadequate when compared to key competitors, evolving customer needs, and so forth.

A good example of "renorming" and its power to evoke change can be seen in the area of personal health. For years Americans equated overall body weight with fitness and health, and those who were not overweight often saw little reason to exercise or make dietary changes. As our society has learned more about such health indicators as percentage of body fat and cholesterol, however, many "normal" weight individuals now have the motivation to exercise, eat right, and make other life-style changes.

In helping to create a new set of norms, middle managers take their cue from top managers, who have in effect redefined good performance at a higher level. Middle managers, then, induce new standards in terms that are meaningful to a specific function. In almost any group, however, there will be strong biases to discount this new assessment.

First, key personnel are likely to feel pride and responsibility for what they see as advantages of the current system. Criticisms of the status quo may be interpreted as personal affronts, and for this reason, existing arrangements are often vigorously defended. It is important for managers to clearly distinguish *individual* performance and responsibility from deficiencies in *organizational* achievement.

Second, negative assessments of current operating performance are also likely to be discounted if they are suddenly imposed on the organization with little or no explanation of the underlying strategic logic. The assessment may be seen as merely a temporary aberration, and operating personnel may actually increase their commitment and redouble their efforts to "prove" the efficacy of the current course.

The key issues involved in creating a need for change within operating units are summarized in the following list.

Creating a Reason for Change

- Provide a new answer to the "How are we doing?" question.
- Avoid personalizing responsibility for the status quo.
- Clarify the logic for change.
- Make the reason permanent.
- Make the long term relevant to operations.

In providing a new answer to the "How are we doing?" question, middle managers must separate personal performance from operating deficiencies and promote shared understanding of the new strategic context. They must provide a logic for the change that has both long-term and operational relevance. In the end, the best approach may be to ask "dumb" questions and engage personnel in discussions that reveal the firm's logic for change in the language of operations.

Like the loan officer encountered by Mr. Terraciano, people need to understand *what* they are doing wrong and, more important, *why* it is wrong. The CEO communicated the new vision, but explaining how it compared with prior practice in the lending group required the intervention of a middle manager. Having developed broad understanding of the inadequacies of current conditions, the organization was then poised to begin charting its future direction.

Strategy into Action

The strategy formulation/implementation dichotomy has tended to advance the perception of implementation as a mechanical, almost bureaucratic, process. In reality, translating strategy into actions is more closely akin to a "learn as you go" process. Even in the most top-down contexts, details of top management's strategy must be fleshed out so that middle managers and operating personnel can formulate a plan of action.

In the action-planning process, middle managers need to be adept at managing two related contradictions. First, they must be both leaders and followers. This means providing clear guidance and, at the same time, tapping into the wisdom of others. Second, to arrive at optimal solutions, middle managers must promote both consensus and conflict. How this takes place varies depending on the leadership style of the manager and the norms of the organization. Whether in formal group settings or in less formal one-on-one conversations, managing these paradoxes is at the heart of effective implementation.

The Two Paradoxes of Implementation

- Managerial Orientations

    Strong leadership
    Sincere followership

- Process Objectives

    Constructive conflict
    Consensus and unity of purpose

Strong, Purposeful Leadership

In getting the organization's attention by reframing the "How are we doing?" question and then using the new answer to facilitate shared understanding of new priorities, the middle manager has begun to provide the leadership necessary for effective implementation. New patterns of thinking evolve slowly, however, and managers are often surprised by how much "misunderstanding" may still exist. More than once, we've heard managers comment, "What's going on? After last week's meeting, I was sure they understood."

The need to reframe performance standards, changing the image members have of the organization (for example, from "we're doing well" to "we're not doing so well"), suggests that there are other unseen barriers to change buried within the minds of organization members. The implementation problem is compounded geometrically, therefore, when successful implementation demands systemwide organization change. Many companies have experienced this difficulty within the context of implementing total quality management (TQM) programs. Experts say that TQM requires a complete metamorphosis and describe the change in thinking as a "paradigm shift."[4] Making this sort of change happen requires a shift both in what members see as the current organizational identity and in their beliefs about the character of the organization.[5]

Middle managers play a key role in creating this type of change for several reasons. First, middle managers are frequently the personification of the organization's current identity. Their central position in the social network makes them the repository for the existing set of beliefs—"the keepers of the paradigm"—and therefore their behavior typically is a model of the dominant social norms. For middle managers, leading change means changing themselves.

Second, middle managers are often the first to recognize or at least fully appreciate the subtleties underlying organizational change. In the synthesizing role, middle managers interact frequently across management levels and external constituencies and, as a result, are continuously reframing the shared understanding held by others about the organization and its circumstances. Boundary-spanning positions, in particular, provide an excellent perspective from which to see the need for change.

Finally, unseating the existing organizational identity and thereby motivating change requires that a new, "ideal" organizational identity be established in the minds of organization members. The gap between ideal and current identities creates a mental discrepancy that motivates people to change.[6] To create this new ideal image and the motivation for change, middle management leaders are well positioned to exploit boundary-spanning practices such as competitive benchmarking and direct customer interaction. Benchmarking changes perceptions by providing real examples of the new performance standards. Direct customer interaction makes members aware of inadequacies in the current organization from an outsider's perspective, and this inevitably causes them to question their views.[7]

To summarize, leading change first means maintaining a dynamic understanding of the gap between the current and ideal organizational identity. Then, to create a motivating discrepancy in the minds of others, middle managers need to use their position as boundary spanners to reshape how the organization sees itself. Creating the needed shift in understanding relies on ongoing dialogues that follow up on critical experiences, such as direct interactions with customers. This cannot be achieved solely in formal action-planning sessions. Throughout the implementation process, as proposals are suggested and discussed, middle managers must constantly remind and reorient people's attention toward underlying concerns and priorities.

In the end, perceptions are based more on managerial actions than on words. In providing the leadership necessary to implement strategic changes, managers must follow through, making real changes in the firm's evaluation and incentive systems or championing these changes when unilateral action is not possible. Reinforcing the importance of emerging concerns and priorities through concrete managerial actions makes them real and motivates people to become involved in substantive action planning.

Inquisitive, Sincere Followership

Although strong leadership represents one side of middle management's role in implementation, the development of action plans for realizing strategic goals relies on the manager's ability to learn from others. Effective middle managers stay in touch with operations themselves, but they still rely on those below them to assess feasibility, identify critical linkages, point out "bottlenecks," and, in general, formulate detailed solutions to strategic issues. Middle management's role is to solicit contributions, ask probing questions, and coordinate diverse inputs into an overall plan that deploys the organization's capability for maximum effect.

Success with subordinates depends largely on the extent to which the manager has respect and credibility. Participative management techniques are often seen as transparent attempts to gain commitment or "placate the troops." In Chapter Four, however, we described how substantive middle management involvement improves the quality of strategic decision making. At the operational level as well, sincere middle management followership means learning from others, exploiting their ideas and talents to improve implementation effectiveness. If the manager has been too removed from operations, lacks appropriate expertise, or seems in any way disingenuous, attempts to solicit input will be seen as a sham and be received cynically. Once again we see the importance of the middle manager's ongoing involvement in operations, and the interconnections among the four strategic roles become apparent.

Constructive Confrontation

In being both a leader and a follower in the implementation process, managers walk a fine line, seeking both constructive debate and consensus. Dangers abound on both sides of this tightrope. On the one hand, in seeking shared understanding and commitment to a new direction, managers run the risk of reducing the number of options considered and prematurely cutting off constructive dialogue. In addition, by exhibiting strong leadership, managers run the risk of telling others "what they want to hear." On the other hand, in their sincere attempts to solicit alternative interpretations and ideas, managers run the risk of being seen as weak and failing to provide direction. Such power vacuums frequently lead to dysfunctional conflict.

Negotiating this course requires (1) making a clear distinction between means (tactics) and ends (objectives) and (2) recognizing that constructive conflict often precedes consensus. Early in the action-planning phase, middle managers should have established a clear sense of the desired objectives in operational terms. This is another place where middle management's ability to translate comes into play. Typically, middle and top managers negotiate these objectives based on top management's overall goals. Subsequent debate should therefore focus on the means for achieving these objectives.

Studies have repeatedly demonstrated that conflict during the decision process generally leads to higher-quality decisions. This realization has led many firms to adopt techniques that actually increase the amount of conflict within a decision team. "Devil's advocates" may be designated, for example, to poke holes in the suggestions and proposals of others.

It will come as no surprise, however, that conflict can damage relationships and, in some cases, do more harm than good. To benefit from conflict without suffering its drawbacks, middle managers at Intel, for example, pioneered the concept of constructive confrontation. Under this system, employees throughout the organization are not only allowed but expected to challenge the ideas of others regardless of their level or position within the firm. Making this the norm and insisting that criticisms remain impersonal diffuses the political land mines that usually lie beneath a confrontational interchange. This allows the best ideas to emerge. At the same time, a shared understanding of the value of conflict in the decision process encourages productive relationships. Within Intel, constructive confrontation is so important that members of top management regularly lead training sessions on it.

Ultimate Commitment and Buy-In

Conflict during the decision process maximizes the number of alternatives considered and holds each one up to careful scrutiny. In the end, however, effective implementation rests on a shared commitment to an agreed-upon course. Thus, while the concept of consensus is often described in process terms, it has great strategic value as an outcome. Seen in this way, strategic consensus represents the level of shared understanding and commitment toward a particular deliberate strategy.

It is simplistic to view strategy as a sequential process moving smoothly from formulation to implementation; however, organizations do move through periods of convergence and divergence.[8] In periods of convergence, basic assumptions and priorities are more or less settled, and the focus is on integrating activities to reach a common objective. In this circumstance, organizations benefit from the efficiency and unity of purpose achieved by strong consensus on strategy and specific actions. During divergent periods, however, strong consensus cuts off the flow of new ideas and creates a form of strategic myopia. The only constructive agreement at this point may be about the need for change itself.

Consensus, then, should be managed in accord with the stage of the decision process. Early in the process, divergence is important, and middle managers should focus the consensus on strategic objectives, with no expectation regarding understanding or commitment to specific action plans. As debate ensues and alternatives are narrowed, consensus should begin to converge on a set of tactics, timetables, and accountabilities.

In the end, no amount of understanding balances a lack of commitment, and too many managers fail to follow through in making changes that affect subordinates' perceptions of how the new strategy affects them. Incentive and reward systems should be redesigned so that contributing to the new plan serves employees' self-interest. Organizational structures may also need revision to best enable the firm to pursue the new course. Our research and that of others[9] suggests that such interventions should be deliberate and purposeful without creating an unnecessary sense of panic. People must be given time to digest new patterns in the strategic logic. Having established the need for change, however, research suggests that participative approaches to action planning and system redesign work best when those participating feel "significant" time pressure.

To summarize, awareness of the need for change is developed gradually through conversations and reorientations in performance standards. Diverse initiatives are proposed and begin to compete for legitimacy. Ultimately, the best of these converge into an integrated set of activities—an action plan. Rapid progress then ensues, as coordinated efforts advance the firm's goals.

Implementation as a Reason to Broaden Middle Management Involvement in Strategy

The point most often misunderstood by top managers is that *middle management implementation effectiveness depends on middle managers' being involved in the other three strategic roles.* Strategic involvement in synthesizing, facilitating, and championing provides middle managers an in-depth understanding of shifting strategic priorities and the underlying rationale for those priorities. Unless middle managers are deeply involved with the levels above them and come to understand the deliberate strategy, how can they implement it?

On the other hand, because implementation means involvement in operations, it affords a realistic view of organizational capabilities and operating circumstances. Involvement in implementation therefore enhances effectiveness in the other three roles. It bears repeating that there is a great deal of interdependence among the four roles, and effective middle managers move from one to the next in an almost seamless series of activities.

Summary

Implementation in the 1990s entails an enormous range of intellectual, leadership, and administrative skills. These can only be acquired as managers experience the diverse challenges embedded in all four strategic roles. There is no shortcut for senior executives who want effective execution. Simply giving subordinates a plan and measuring performance against a set of goals will not work. Executives who fail to embrace broad-based, strategic involvement are likely to be stuck with an unrealized plan.

Part Three

Unleashing the Power in the Middle

Chapter Nine

The Challenge of Executive Leadership

We believe middle managers will continue to play a vital role in the future of large organizations. Indeed, we see their level of influence and importance increasing, not decreasing. Leveraging core capability is at the heart of organization strategy, and the four middle management roles we have described are intimately linked to the firm's capability accumulation and deployment process. Without middle managers, firms are likely to lose the ability to reinvent themselves, build new capabilities, and remain competitive.

But how does our view fit with prophecies declaring the extinction of middle managers?[1] Much of the apparent confusion stems from how middle managers have been defined and how their work has been interpreted. Traditionally, middle managers have held line authority over some function or subfunction within the organization's overall structure. For the most part, their work has been viewed as "making sure other people perform" (controlling) and serving as conduits of communication.

Reengineering designs work away from vertical functions toward horizontal processes. Thus job titles, work relationships, and responsibilities change. In the end, however, there remains the need for individuals adept at managing the formation of strategy from within the organization. These are the middle managers of the future. In the preface, we defined middle management broadly as "any individual who is regularly involved in, or interfaces with, the organization's operations and who has some access to upper management." In subsequent chapters we elaborated the unique significance of this position and described the potential for value-adding, strategic contributions from individuals located in the middle of the organization.

In this chapter we examine the design of reengineered organizations in light of middle management's strategic potential and describe the importance of executive leadership to the realization of that potential. There are several objectives here. First, we want to be explicit about our assumptions regarding the evolving shape of large organizations. We agree there is a shift toward horizontal processes and fewer managerial layers, but this hardly rings a death knell for middle management. Second, we want to provide top management with a new way of thinking about and pursuing restructuring. The benefits of restructuring come from tapping the potential of those in the middle of the organization, and this requires top managers who have a clear understanding of the relationship between organizational capability and middle management behavior.

The Evolving Design of Large Organizations: Taking the Middle Out?

No one denies that a hierarchy can be dysfunctional. Authority can get out of hand, and many organizations have acquired too many layers. The centralization and rigidity associated with overly layered organizations stifles involvement, innovation, and leadership. It is fundamentally wrong, however, to equate hierarchy with outdated management systems or to assume that all hierarchy is bad.

Accountability and Authority Differences

The question of how many layers of management are appropriate for any given organization is only partly a matter of structuring work, in other words, whether tasks will be centered within functional departments or within processes consisting of cross-functional teams. An equally important issue is accountability.

"Hierarchy is the only form of organization that can enable a company to employ large numbers of people and yet preserve unambiguous accountability."[2] As Elliott Jaques observes, ours is a culture where individuals, not groups, are held accountable by employers. The employment contract is between you and the company, not between your team and the company. Groups or teams may reach agreement about decisions, but ultimately individuals are held accountable. If no one is left with the authority to either approve or disapprove of group decisions, accountability disappears. In the end, organizations are left with hierarchy as the only means for ensuring accountability, and authority distinctions between layers result directly from this fact.

To be appropriate, the number of layers should be consistent with natural breaks in the time horizon of problems and decisions facing various managerial positions. According to Jaques these breaks occur at three months, one year, two years, five years, ten years, and twenty years. With increases in time span come differences in mental capacity and breadth of perspective, and this provides a basis for differentiating accountability.

One problem is that organizations have confused the need for differences in pay with the need for hierarchy, thereby creating unnecessary and dysfunctional authority distinctions based on pay grade. In addition, many organizations have ignored elements of design that enhance interpersonal relationships, foster reciprocity, and create flexibility, including, most important, the need for shared values and interpersonal trust. But no one expects accountability to go away, and neither will hierarchy.

Consider the organizational design of one of the country's most progressive companies. Motorola utilizes a network of hierarchical committees as the infrastructure for its highly successful participative management program (PMP). Innovation, and the involvement that fuels it, is the company's lifeblood, but decisions must be made and resources committed in order to act on the ideas coming from the teams. Each team has one of its members on a committee at the next highest level. Besides coordinating and communicating ideas, it is the hierarchy that controls implementation by negotiating standards and measures of performance. Rewards are indeed shared by teams (in proportion to individual salary), and there are only four levels between the shop floor and the chief executive. But as a premise of their organization, Motorola identifies team *managers* as the ones who are accountable for drawing out ideas and using them to solve business problems.[3]

Clearly, reengineering does not bring about the end of hierarchy. Who will lead the process-owning team? Who will measure and evaluate the performance of subprocess teams? Who will lead the steering committees? Who will these people report to? *Anyone who has ever attempted to set up an "unstructured" work team knows that the first thing these teams do is create a structure.* People—individuals— must be held accountable for making the reengineering process work. Like anything else, if an individual fails, someone else will be assigned the task.

Task Complexity and Team Differences

Moreover, there are differing levels of complexity in the tasks assigned to teams. A team that is responsible for an entire process (for example, from order to fulfillment) has a much more complex job, with more variables and more interrelationships, than a team that is responsible for a subprocess. These differences in complexity track closely with differences in time span responsibility, and they are going to be reflected in the status and authority of team managers. It is doubtful, for example, that top management teams will ever put themselves on a par with operating teams, nor should they.

Looking carefully at a reengineered organization, such as Texas Instruments, one sees processes instead of functions as the main division of work, and one sees fewer layers from top to bottom. But there are still layers, and those teams in the middle are led by middle managers. In fact, some teams are composed entirely of middle managers![4]

Thus the need for accountability and the differences in the time span and complexity of work make hierarchical layers inevitable in large organizations. The number of layers may decline and their formal responsibilities may change, but middle managers do not disappear.

Information Technology as an Enabler

Information technology (IT) is commonly identified as a key "enabler" of delayering and is sometimes seen as an important reason on its own for the elimination of middle management. Many would argue that IT changes everything, making accountability and time span arguments obsolete. The empirical evidence on the effects of IT are far more subtle, however.

A recent study of the research on IT and middle management summarized the cumulative findings as a paradox: IT both increases and decreases the number of middle managers.[5] The authors observe that decentralization is what influences which way IT's effect on middle management goes. When an organization is highly centralized, middle management is limited to its operating roles (information and control), and IT is highly "substitutable" for these activities. Hence the number of middle managers declines in a centralized environment.

In a decentralized organization, on the other hand, "middle manager's roles are mainly decisional, and decisions are unstructured and non-routine."[6] In our terms, the key middle manager roles are the strategic ones. In general, the use of IT enhances not decreases middle management's value. With more advanced technology at their disposal, middle managers become more important to the organization, and all else being equal, this tends to increase their number.

Needless to say, decentralization is far more compatible with the goals of reengineering, and when coupled with the effective use of IT the results can be dramatic. At a Cleveland-based machine tool company, for example, decentralization has been carried to its logical conclusion: plant managers are being treated as though they were chief executives. The company has pushed decision-making authority down as far down as possible, holding plant managers accountable for both customer responsiveness and profitability. In conjunction with these new responsibilities, computers play a key role in "informating" plant foremen and supervisors. Data about costs, downtime, and customer needs, which used to be channeled back to headquarters, now go directly to plant management. The result has been a dramatic reduction in order-to-fulfillment cycle time, in one plant from twelve weeks down to just a few days. In addition, happy customers have increased the company's backlog by 30 percent.[7]

In the early 1980s, it was popular to think of information technology as a way for top executives to run the business directly, without the information filtering and distortion created by middle management. Armed with an executive information system, the computer terminal became a "dashboard" through which senior managers monitored unit performance and communicated direction to the troops. This vision, which some firms actually tried to realize, was based on an obsession with concentration of authority and control at the top. The approach also made naive assumptions about the information needed to make sound decisions.

Nevertheless, U.S. manufacturing companies invested millions on systems designed to report inventories, production levels, and plant costs to top management. Observing the lack of IT sophistication in Japan, American managers firmly believed that such technology was a means of regaining their competitive edge. Instead, while U.S. managers were trying to control inventory, the Japanese eliminated it. Working with information coming from teams at the operating level, Japanese middle managers negotiated delivery of inventory from suppliers and between production units "just in time" (JIT) to meet the need. In sharp contrast to the dashboard approach, JIT was based on pushing decision-making authority down to the middle and bottom layers, those closest to the information. The American investment in elaborate production/inventory control has proven in many cases to be not an advantage but a "competitive burden."[8]

Even relying on IT to automate middle management's operating roles risks a degree of centralization and over-control that can undermine a company's ability to adapt to change. As we have argued, organizations need middle managers to synthesize information, facilitate adaptability, and champion new initiatives, and no one has suggested that IT can automate this. Americans in particular are too easily enamored with sophisticated technology and tend to see it as a panacea for management problems.[9] In short, the idea that middle managers can be replaced by information technology is simply part of the mythology that has surrounded the restructuring movement.

Delayering by Design: Linking Restructuring to Middle Management Behavior

So, middle management remains an important feature of restructured firms. But what criteria should top management use to decide which managers remain and, perhaps more important, what these managers should do? We hope that by now the reader has become convinced that this is a strategic question, a key challenge facing senior management. This is an issue too important to be left to the random influences of attrition or across-the-board incentives and cutbacks.

First and foremost, top managers must explicitly consider their objectives for restructuring. Is the effort being precipitated by an organizational crisis? Is it a strategic adjustment designed to offer the firm a new way of competing? Whether they view restructuring as the source of a new competitive advantage or as a strategic necessity, the firm's executive leadership must tie the goals of restructuring to the organizational capabilities they hope to achieve.

For most firms today, these capabilities center on innovation and customer responsiveness. Within every firm, however, these broad terms mean something different and must be precisely defined in a way that is strategically meaningful. Firms must be precise about the types of innovation they will seek to exploit and the areas of responsiveness important to their customers.

Having linked restructuring to desired capabilities, it becomes important to recognize the integral connection between capability and the middle management resource base. Those areas where innovation and creativity are desired, for example, are perhaps best served by middle managers predisposed to facilitating and championing. Alternatively, elements of the organization facing serious strategic uncertainty are suited to managers with strong synthesizing skills. Finally, for most firms there will be areas of operation marked by little uncertainty, dynamism, or complexity, and here effective implementation capabilities are paramount.

In a nutshell then, restructuring decisions cannot be made at a general, universal level. Each activity within the organization must be considered for its contribution to desired organizational competencies. Individual competencies and predispositions can then be identified and channeled in a way that supports the objectives of the restructuring effort.

Middle Management Involvement: The Key to Successful Reengineering

By being explicit about the logic underlying the restructuring effort, top management is better positioned to face its biggest challenge, getting middle management input in a process that threatens established positions. Such input is critical since top managers see the organization's design in highly abstract terms, usually in terms of how boxes are arranged on an organization chart. Middle managers, on the other hand, see the design in more detailed, concrete terms—as specific people who make particular contributions.

Rearranging the boxes at the top, even when the rearrangement is actually "implemented," will not lead to the kind of deep structural change senior management is pursuing in the reengineering effort. No amount of care by staff members in redefining unit responsibilities, job titles, and individual accountabilities will make a difference if the process of organization design is entirely top-down. Indeed, changing words on paper to effect a change in work is a bureaucratic approach doomed to fail because it overlooks the need for commitment by those who are affected.

Nevertheless, the number of companies who have pursued this centralized, myopic approach to restructuring is legion. It is perpetuated by the assumption that middle and operating-level managers are simply not up to the challenge. The experience of a regional telephone company provides a useful illustration.

Like many of the "Baby Bells," the phone company we studied had struggled over the last decade to adjust to the deregulated, highly competitive environment of telecommunications. The bureaucratic way of doing things created under conditions of monopoly was deeply rooted in the culture of the company, and despite several rounds of downsizing, the company continued to lose ground in most of its businesses.

Senior managers, of course, were well aware of the problem they faced, and in 1991 the company announced a major organizational restructuring. Several thousand positions were eliminated, but management also declared that there was a "new way of doing business." A new senior vice president for finance was hired away from one of the long distance competitors and put in charge of the restructuring plans. Working with consultants, senior management developed a radically new and highly progressive organization structure that was communicated to all managers via an organization chart. Top management was on the bottom, each of the business units was shown as an autonomous entity, and the principle of teams was emphasized by the inclusion of a circle in which three individuals were identified as the "office of the president." Middle managers in business units were charged with creating similar structures and reporting back to headquarters.

The new organization chart had virtually no impact on the company's modus operandi. Instead, middle and operating-level managers greeted it somewhat cynically as "public relations." In the words of one manager: "The organization chart has no relationship at all to the bureaucracy that exists, and by downsizing, all that management has accomplished is to make us even less efficient and more unresponsive to the market." Clearly, top management failed to get buy-in for the new structure. How could they? The process provided no real opportunity for middle and operating levels to get involved until after the key decisions had already been made.

Most managers know that buy-in only comes with involvement. But because restructuring threatens job security, this rule does not seem to apply. Instead, the dominant approach is that top management creates the restructuring template in secrecy, announcing it only after key guidelines—such as the definition of core processes and percentage head count reduction—have been determined.

Fixing such basic variables gives middle managers very little flexibility in how they respond to the need for change. In fact, eliminating flexibility is exactly the point. The vast majority of top managers believe there is no other way to ensure compliance. In a recent survey, for example, 94 percent of responding top executives believe that middle managers do not completely comply with business objectives.[10] Ironically, one of the primary reasons why middle managers are out of sync with objectives comes from a failure to understand what those objectives are. In fact, most of the managers we surveyed in a 1990 study could not identify their president's top priority. Similarly, a Harris poll found that less than a third of employees think top management provides clear goals and direction.[11]

Reaching Consensus on Restructuring

Nevertheless, reaching consensus—creating a shared understanding and commitment among management—is necessary before a restructuring strategy can be executed effectively. Otherwise, middle managers who are not committed to the action will try to undermine it, dragging their feet and even sabotaging attempts to reduce expenses. Middle managers continue to have great discretion in most companies, despite some attempts to limit it, because top managers rely on them to make things work. This discretion combined with lack of commitment accounts for the common gap between top management's restructuring goals and reality.

Commitment is built on a detailed understanding of the strategy, not merely an understanding that "reducing costs is all that matters," or that "headcount must decrease by 30 percent." Middle managers need to understand the "whys," and top managers should work toward consensus by getting middle levels involved from the start, *before* the numbers are cast in stone. Decisions about what the new structure should look like and about headcount should be made only after involving those who are closest both to the customer and operations. This provides the kind of input needed to get beyond the superficial, overly abstract rearrangement of the boxes on the organization chart. Accumulating this information from operating levels and synthesizing it in meaningful ways requires middle managers who understand the complexities of the bigger picture.

Once top managers get over the assumption that the elimination of most middle managers is a necessary part of restructuring, there is a foundation for constructive dialogue and for closing the trust gap between the two layers. Mistrust is perpetuated by top management secrecy and by middle managers who hold top management hostage to critical information. Sharing information begins when top management recognizes that middle managers will continue to play a vital role—even if some middle managers, along with some top managers and operating personnel, must ultimately leave the corporation.

In 1989, the exploration and production division of Sun Company[12] was facing the need for an organizational restructuring to do away with management layers and a cumbersome bureaucracy. Low oil prices had become a permanent condition rather than a temporary blip in the U.S. economy. Top management called in groups of managers and described the tough times facing the company. Generous severance was offered to anyone volunteering to leave, and some able managers opted to go. Two hundred of the remaining middle managers were formed into teams and asked to analyze company operations. One group, for example, found that records on the ownership of wells were kept in fourteen separate locations.

Tracing such inefficiencies made it abundantly clear just how important the reorganization was. "Suddenly we had two hundred evangelists," according to the division president, James McCormick.

The payoffs in commitment from this open approach have been significant. As McCormick puts it: "Every employee who is here knows we want them here, and we know they wanted to stay. That has made all the difference." In addition, the way restructuring was handled set a precedent that encourages continuing frank discussions of company strategy. In the words of a geoscientist at Sun: "People are a lot more willing to sign on if you tell them the business reasons for doing something."

Thus, the likelihood of employee separations should not limit the level of involvement that accompanies the restructuring process. The lack of information and resulting mistrust lead to cynicism rather than consensus about the strategy, and under these conditions middle management is likely to undermine senior management's goals. Research suggests that participation works even when it comes to deciding who should stay and who should go. Using rewards such as early retirements, severance plans, benefits extensions, and outplacements, the touchiest of restructuring issues can be confronted in an atmosphere of open information sharing.[13]

A High-Involvement Approach to Restructuring: Steps in the Process

Top management should think of restructuring as a major strategic change. Like all significant change, successful restructuring relies on the involvement of middle managers and other organization members. We devote the last section of this chapter to key points in management's strategy for restructuring. At a broader level, these same ideas serve as guidelines to top managers who are interested in harnessing middle management resources in the pursuit of *any* strategy.

Recognize the link between competitive advantage, core capability, and middle management. Reengineering should occur with an acute awareness of the company's advantages and the capabilities underlying them. In many firms, restructuring is a response to a competitive crisis where costs are grossly out of line and/or customer satisfaction has deteriorated. In the process of discovering the reasons for such problems, top managers may find their perceptions about competitive advantage out of date. Indeed, the fact that there is a crisis is evidence of an obsolete strategy. Nevertheless, proceeding with restructuring in the absence of a clear idea about its effects on competitive advantage risks losing the knowledge, skill base, and social relationships that compose the underlying capability.

Identifying a firm's competitive advantage is no easy task, but in most cases at least, there is external, objective evidence (such as customer surveys) to help in the process. Perhaps more challenging is the self-examination required to uncover the organizational capabilities that create the advantage.

We worked with one of the world's largest insurers of industrial plant and equipment. The company is known for its financial stability and expertise in evaluating industrial risks. Like many casualty insurers, its claims experience during the first half of the 1990s was terribly adverse due to a series of natural disasters: California earthquakes, hurricane Andrew, and unusually severe winter weather. These events and new pressures to be price competitive precipitated organizational restructuring as a means to cut costs.

Initially, senior management believed that the firm's most fundamental advantage lay in its detailed underwriting procedure. The headquarters underwriting function had spent literally decades formalizing and documenting the guidelines for assuming risk, and the company considered the resulting proprietary system a key advantage. When it came to restructuring, therefore, top management had reached the decision to exempt the staff responsible for applying the system and to direct most of the cuts at the field sales force.

As is typical in restructuring, the regional managers were called into headquarters to discuss how they could "contribute" to the cost cutting. At this point, the authors were engaged to explain middle management's "roles in the planning process." Instead of formal planning, we helped facilitate a broader discussion of why the company had seen an erosion in its market share.

In the process of this dialogue, it became apparent that rigid underwriting procedures and lack of binding authority in the field sales force had created an opportunity for competitors. In fact, had it not been for the technical expertise and market sensitivity in regional sales offices, the share erosion would have been even more dramatic. As senior management spent more time talking with regional vice presidents, awareness grew about this source of advantage. Ultimately, cuts had to be made, but the focus on cost savings was redirected in order to preserve the regional selling and underwriting expertise as a core capability.

Frequently, the link between what the organization does and its competitive advantage is quite ambiguous and often misunderstood even by senior level executives.[14] The reason for this is that those most intimately associated with the capability are positioned within operations and are disconnected from the strategic environment, while those who know the strategy are unfamiliar with the detail of internal working arrangements. If anyone knows the link between operations and strategy, it is middle-level managers. The key, therefore, is to get them involved in the process of defining core capability.

Identify middle managers with the requisite skills, experiences, and potential to thrive within the new organization. Once management has developed a consensus about what the core capabilities are or should be, it is easier to differentiate the relative value added by various subunits. The logic here is similar to that used in making outsourcing decisions. There are key areas of capability where the firm now adds value (or should) in ways that differentiate it from competitors, and there are other areas of capability that are necessary and important but do not contribute to competitive advantage.

In building a restructuring strategy, differentiating among middle managers in this way is absolutely vital. It is important first because the knowledge of those who manage and operate the key subunits is needed to correct the strategic misalignment that created the need for restructuring in the first place. To restructure effectively, one is likely to need a new strategy as well as a new structure. Second, it is important so that the downsizing knife avoids cutting in core areas. Even when the staff reductions are voluntary, the goal is to lose as little capability as possible. And third, distinguishing among managers and subunits is important to the people involved. Nothing is worse than uncertainty, and nothing inspires less confidence than arbitrary, across-the-board cutbacks. Making the tough decisions based on input from those affected sends a strong signal that management understands the problems and is moving to correct them. In many ways this is the toughest step in the process, but the longer senior managers delay the dialogue about core capabilities and the needed changes, the worse problems will become.

It must have seemed like the problems could not get any worse at Zeneca Agricultural Products (a unit of Britain's Imperial Chemical Industries).[15] Profits were down, price competition was up, and inventories were a disaster. In the midst of all this, the subsidiary was being spun off, and its president, Bob Woods, faced the real prospect that corporate-level management would decide to divest the business. Meetings with his executive team produced predictable rounds of finger-pointing. So Woods went around the executive ranks and appointed teams of middle-level managers to work on redefining the business according to a "customer friendly" architecture. Needless to say, many of the executives were infuriated, but the process took on a life of its own. Soon, both Woods and most of his executives were spending all their time with the new teams. The turnaround was so rapid that head count reductions needed to be much less than expected (around 10 percent). More important, Woods had a management team that knew what its advantages were, and this provided the best context for ongoing change. Said Woods, "You don't know the endpoint, though you try to convince people you really do know. . . . you have to have faith."

The Zeneca story illustrates why many top managers resort to overseeing random attrition and across-the-board cutbacks rather than lead a true restructuring process. People need to be involved, but early in the process a powerful minority of middle managers or executives is likely to become a stumbling block. These are usually the managers who think they stand to lose power and who have power because they once were the locus of the company's advantage.

The strategy Bob Woods used is instructive. First, he insisted that decisions be made at the middle and operating levels, down where the customer and technical contact is most intense. Second, he allowed the naysayers to stand on the sidelines until they were ready to accept the need for change. Once the train leaves the station and the new course is set, most of the key managers will join in. Those that don't are left behind. For those who are aboard, however, there are new expectations. This leads to the third key point in the restructuring process.

See that the organization is redesigned to leverage the abilities of key middle managers and encourage their influence on strategic priorities.

Restructuring requires leadership at the middle as well as the top of the organization. It is up to those who have the most power to see to it that the champions of change below are brought to the surface, rewarded, and extended formal authority. Sometimes this means leapfrogging the existing hierarchy, but this is a case where being bashful is likely to allow a last-gasp resurrection by the obsolete power structure. Old ways die hard, and the chief executive is likely to be the only person in a position to give the new cadre needed legitimacy. Do it sooner rather than later.

It is equally important, however, not to lose sight of the fact that nothing is forever. Restructuring is an ongoing process, and the goal is to create a continuously self-designing organization. Concentrating power too much in the hands of a few—even if they are "process owners"—can lead to a new set of tyrants. By encouraging initiative and involvement at *all* levels, there is a chance that the rigor mortis of organizational inertia can be avoided.

Involving middle managers in a strategy-driven reengineering process is the only way top managers can avoid sacrificing core capabilities and competitive advantage in an effort to control costs and serve the customer better. More important, reengineering is not a "once and for all" kind of process. Top managers must build in a dynamic capability that fosters continuous refinement and redesign of the organization. Middle managers are crucial to this process.

Summary

Restructuring is here to stay. It is, on the whole, a healthy response to a fundamentally changed set of business conditions. Restructuring, however, does not mark the end of middle management. Indeed, middle management's strategic roles are accentuated within the restructured firm. Successful restructuring requires careful consideration of the linkage between organizational goals and middle management skill and capability. Involving middle managers in the restructuring process establishes the logic, commitment, and understanding necessary for successful management of the restructured firm.

Chapter Ten

Becoming a Strategic Middle Manager

When we talk to middle managers about their involvement in strategy, they readily appreciate the importance of the four strategic roles. Almost all report spending less time on championing, facilitating, and synthesizing activities than they would like, however. Overall it seems that most managers spend less than a quarter of their time in the four strategic roles.

Figure 10.1 presents the results of a study we conducted among 275 middle managers from twenty-five organizations. These graphs reveal that most middle managers either never or, at best, only occasionally participate in the firm's strategic process. Just as telling, the graphs show that only a minority of middle managers, around 10 percent, influence strategy very regularly.

What is not shown in these tables is that the pattern of involvement varies among organizations. Reported levels of involvement were significantly higher for managers in the sample's eight most innovative firms. In addition, our evidence suggests that performance in the roles is key to the realization of organizational strategy and that higher levels of involvement improve financial performance.

We can draw at least two conclusions. First, on the whole it seems that middle managers do not give enough attention to the strategic side of their work. Judging from widespread complaints about the lack of innovation and flexibility in organizations, everyone would like to see more championing, facilitating, and synthesizing behavior. Second, a small minority of middle managers appear to be much more influential than others. These

Figure 10.1. Middle Managers' Self-Reports of Their Strategic Activity.

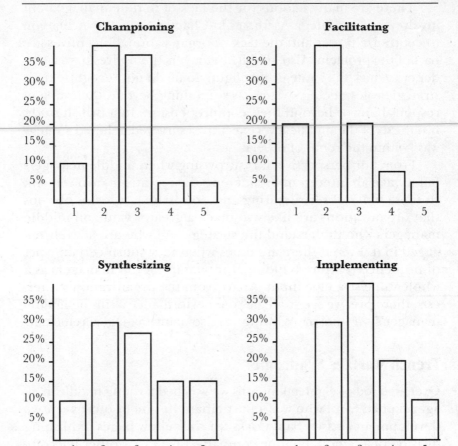

Championing

Facilitating

Synthesizing

Implementing

	K	E	Y	
1= Never	**2**= Rarely	**3**= Occasionally	**4**= Regularly	**5**= Frequently

managers represent the lifeblood of the firm's dynamic capability, but they appear to be in short supply.

There are many reasons for the lack of middle management involvement in strategy. As we saw in Chapter Nine, the inclination to centralize power and the lack of organizational incentives are part of the problem. Also, middle managers themselves have a tendency to duck the strategic limelight. Some do not recognize their strategic roles, seeing strategy as something beyond their area of responsibility or beyond their comprehension. In a British study, two-thirds of the middle-level executives surveyed believed strategy was "within the remit of others."[1]

From our perspective, it is surprising when middle managers fail to take an interest in broadening their strategic involvement. In these times of restructuring and downsizing, it seems obvious that organizations are likely to place a greater value on middle managers who understand the strategy and who are actively engaged in it. Even if there are times when they spurn certain types of influence (empire building, for example), top managers as a whole value strategic input. Apart from the organization's interests, therefore, we see strategic role performance as in the middle manager's *self*-interest. Why then are so many managers reluctant?

Trench Warfare Syndrome

Over a period of eighteen months we watched a young middle manager named Sam, who was a participant in one of our executive development classes. Sam works for the yellow pages publishing division of a regional phone company. Like many other telecommunications firms, the company had been undergoing tumultuous restructuring. Thousands of positions had been eliminated, mostly at middle and operating levels, and like many survivors, Sam's attitude toward the company had become quite hostile.

His work behavior followed a withdrawal pattern we have seen before. Call it the "trench warfare syndrome." Maintaining a low profile and "keeping your nose clean" (in other words, avoiding any hint of disagreement) is the best way to survive. Getting involved in discussions about strategy is sticking your neck out, and organizational politics are such that the enemy is as likely to be a colleague as a superior.

Ironically, the "hunker down" posture makes one an easy target. It fulfills everyone's stereotype of the do-nothing middle manager. When the ax falls, managers in the trenches rarely see it coming.

Sam and a team of colleagues were assigned a study of the organizational processes in his division. The group uncovered a set of symptoms one might expect in a once-regulated company: too much centralization, functional myopia, and obsolete technologies. Using concepts from the course, the analysis led to a set of recommendations that Sam thought management should listen to. He was disappointed when a copy of the report he had sent to his manager got no response.

Nine months later, the company hired a new president. Coming from a distinctly customer-focused consumer products firm, her first order of business was to streamline the bureaucracy. A series of management presentations were offered on the principles of reengineering. Sam immediately recognized the relevance of his group's report. He made another copy of the document and sent it to his boss (a direct-report of the president). This time the analysis and recommendations got some attention, so much so that Sam was asked to lead one of the newly formed reengineering teams.

In a subsequent conversation, Sam's attitude about work had changed. "Now, I can see some direction . . . some awareness at the top about what the problems are and what needs to be done. . . . If nothing else, being in charge of reengineering puts me in a good position to survive!" Although there was still a tinge of sarcasm in Sam's voice, he had come out of the trenches and become an active participant in his company's strategic process.

We have found two things that appear to make the difference in middle managers' willingness or ability to be involved in a strategic role: appropriate knowledge and needed skills. Sam's story illustrates both. The remainder of this chapter has two objectives: first, to detail the challenges of becoming strategically involved, and second, to offer some suggestions for overcoming them.

Knowing Your Organization's Strategy

Most middle managers lack any real knowledge of their organization's strategy. Sam had concluded that his company didn't have a strategy, and in our research we have routinely received similar responses. When we ask middle managers to express their organization's strategy in two or three sentences, for example, the response is often a blank stare. Of those who do respond, most relate strategy in purely financial terms. "Improve return on investment" is easily the most popular phrase over hundreds of responses.

To constructively influence strategy, middle managers must have an understanding that goes beyond financial objectives. In particular, they should take responsibility for understanding strategy from three distinct perspectives. First, they should understand the firm's business from the perspective of key external constituents, including customers, suppliers, and competitors. Second, they should have a thorough understanding of operating realities: what the firm is and is not capable of and what operating priorities currently exist. Third, managers should come to understand the business from the perspective of top management. What are the objectives of the top executive and other members of the top management team? How satisfied are they? In what directions do they see the business evolving? Middle managers should regularly be asking themselves these questions, and if they do not know the answers, their first priority should be to find them. The outline below summarizes how to build an understanding of strategy. Readers may also want to refer to the "Elements of the Strategic Knowledge Base" in Chapter Six to refresh their memories about the *content* of a firm's knowledge base.

Learning Strategy from Three Perspectives

- The external perspective

   Pay attention and expect surprises.
   Work beyond organization boundaries.

- The operational perspective

   Define strategic significance of core activities (across functions).
   Relate activities to distinctive competencies.
   Identify key coordinating mechanisms.

- The top management perspective

   Have deliberate conversations.
   Administer the Strategic Consensus Questionnaire.

Tracking the External Context

Several years ago we conducted an intensive study on the levels of strategic understanding among top and middle-level managers in a medium-size commercial bank. To us it seemed as though management were living in another era, except for the new president and marketing vice president who were trying to create an improved marketing orientation. The whole team had grown up in a regulated environment, and with more than fifty branches, the bank enjoyed a largely unchallenged niche of depositors with low to moderate incomes. But despite three years of growing competitive pressures and an increasing likelihood of takeover, management's approach to the business still had hardly changed. Some of the managers seemed proud of their "stay the course" strategy. They were aware of, and acknowledged, the new president's customer-service orientation, but most seemed happier with a "hunker down" mentality.

Despite readily available sources of information (including plenty of *American Banker* articles written during the past three years calling on banks to be more market and service oriented), the middle managers in the bank had not educated themselves on the bank's strategic external circumstances. They had even avoided serious or sustained contact with customers. As a consequence, they were unmotivated and unable to influence the need for a change in strategy. Rather than being a force for innovation, they had become the source of obfuscation and inertia.

Unfortunately, the tendency to become complacent, to see things as they *were* rather than as they *are,* is a consequence of being human. In light of our limitations, what can a middle manager do to avoid becoming part of organizational inertia?[2]

Pay attention and expect surprises. How is it possible that we are often able to tell middle managers things they did not know about their own industry but that we learned simply from reading the annual report? Not only company documents but newspapers, magazines, trade journals, and the like are full of vital information about industry trends and even company strategies. It is important not to filter out or discount information that is inconsistent with prior beliefs, however. That is inertia creeping in. Look for and expect surprises, not validation of existing patterns. Remember, strategy is about adapting to the future, not living in the past.

Work beyond the organization's boundaries. Frequently, outsider perspectives are a key source of divergent ideas that become the foundation of a changing strategy. Yet customers, suppliers, competitors, consultants, financial analysts, and other outsiders are likely to be under-represented in a manager's knowledge base unless he makes deliberate attempts to include them. Knowledge that spans organizational boundaries is incredibly powerful inside the management hierarchy. Successful top managers know this and rely heavily on networks of outsiders to build their knowledge base. The same applies to middle-level strategy makers.

At the extreme, going outside for knowledge may mean leaving the company. Ironically, "if you stay with a company too long, you get taken for granted. . . . Changing employers can provide broader knowledge and state-of-the-art skills"[3] The value of bringing someone new into the organization is not simply one of perception. Hiring from the outside can be an important way to shortcut the learning process and introduce valuable divergence into management thinking.

Failure to pay attention and seek input outside the organization leaves one unaware of key contextual variables that account for the organization's strategy. Who are the major competitors? Who are the customers and what are their needs? Where will technology be in the next century? These are the questions strategy makers struggle with. Ignoring them makes it very difficult to understand and contribute to the process.

Becoming Intimate with Operations

Managers should come to know their firm's strategy from the operational perspective. In brief, this means managers need to understand the technical and social activities that take place to deliver the product or service to the customer.

This does not mean becoming myopic. The strategic perspective is a broad one, and even functional managers should look at things as if they were general managers. They should understand the cost and strategic significance of each of the firm's core activities. Such understanding should extend beyond the manager's functional specialization.

In more specific terms, middle managers should strive to identify and understand those competencies that are unique or distinctive to the firm. What is it that the firm does particularly well? Understanding these strengths provides a basis for linking operations to strategy and competencies to appropriate opportunities. It is fundamental, therefore, to middle management championing and to a large degree determines management's overall ability to lead the firm in new directions.

As important, managers need to understand how the technical skills and competencies of individuals and subunits are coordinated into organization-level competencies. This knowledge of operational-level managerial capabilities is critical for assessing the firm's dynamic capability and identifying what additional potential competencies the firm might realistically acquire. In many respects, the prescription for gaining an operating-level understanding of strategy is similar to that prescribed for the external environment: pay attention, have deliberate conversations, and work beyond *intra*-organizational (functional) boundaries.

Understanding Top Management Priorities

Finally, to have strategic influence one has to understand top management's priorities. Otherwise, there is no way to judge when the timing is right to advance a proposal, or even whether an initiative is in the ballpark. Yet in case after case we find that middle managers have only a rudimentary understanding of how top management perceives the strategic issues in their company, much less what its strategy is.

In some cases, turmoil or indecision at the top can make priorities difficult to discern. But as we have tried to suggest in the synthesizing discussion, middle managers have a responsibility to know, understand, and even influence top management's view of strategy.

There cannot be meaningful strategic conversation between management levels until there is a shared strategic understanding of the context and the basic strategy. The good news is that involvement and shared understanding are mutually reinforcing. Once Sam was listened to, he was willing and able to become more involved and assumed a position of strategic leadership that enabled him to learn even more about the firm's strategy.

Administering the Strategic Consensus Questionnaire

In addition to each individual manager learning about strategy from the external, internal, and top management perspectives, we suggest the whole management team "go to school" on the company strategy.[4] Resource A is a questionnaire used in our consulting and research projects.[5] The items measure management's strategic priorities: roughly how much emphasis is put on dimensions of differentiation and cost leadership in competitive strategy. (The survey works best at the business or strategic business unit level of analysis, but it can be used even within a department.) Permission is granted to make several copies of this resource for internal nonprofit use within your company.

First give the survey to your boss, or your boss's boss, including the division manager or president of the company. Then, without looking at their responses, fill out the survey yourself. You will also want to distribute the survey to other middle managers or to your own subordinates. Be careful to tell people, especially subordinates, that the survey is anonymous and that you are not "testing" their knowledge of strategy. We have found that people are often afraid to respond to such a survey, for fear of "being wrong."[6]

When you have finished collecting the data, create a grid representing the overall importance of cost or differentiation for each of the responses. (A key for creating this score is in the resource.) Depending on the need for anonymity, you can represent each person with some meaningful identifier, or simply show each person as a dot.

Patterns of Understanding and Commitment in a Commercial Bank

Figure 10.2 shows consensus maps for the commercial bank we described earlier in the chapter. The example illustrates how consensus maps can be used not only to assess the amount of understanding in a firm but also for identifying sources of confusion. Figure 10.2a shows that the newly appointed president and a few other managers saw the strategy as a "hybrid," combining strong emphasis on differentiation and cost. Most of the functional managers, however, saw the strategy as cost driven. Not surprisingly, marketing managers were exceptions, believing differentiation to

Figure 10.2. Shared Understanding and Commitment in a Commercial Bank.

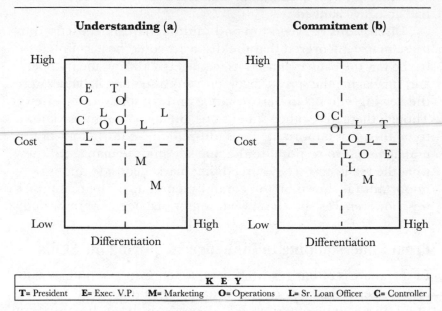

K E Y
T= President   **E**= Exec. V.P.   **M**= Marketing   **O**= Operations   **L**= Sr. Loan Officer   **C**= Controller

Source: Floyd and Wooldrige, "Managing Strategic Consensus: the Foundation of Effect Implementation," *The Executive,* vol. IV, 4, p. 27. Reprinted by permission.

be most important. Thus the consensus map shows that the CEO's strategic intent was not well understood—middle managers did not believe differentiation was a high priority.

Consistent with these results, the CEO communicated concern that many managers in the bank didn't recognize the new competitive realities and were not responding to the need for better customer service and more new products. Why?

Part of the explanation came from comparing managers' perceptions of what the strategy *was* with their perceptions of what it *should be*. Notice that the second figure (10.2b) is an indicator of *commitment* to the strategies. We measured this by asking each person what they thought the priorities should be, aside from what they said priorities were. This approach often helps to clarify the source of confusion, and in this case, functional and top managers expressed more agreement about what should be than what was.

In other words, many of the firm's managers recognized the need to change priorities; they simply did not believe that the priorities had actually changed.

Discussions between top and middle managers, focused by these maps, uncovered that the disparity could be accounted for by the way the bank evaluated its managers. "Making the numbers" and "managing the spread" between bank assets and liabilities were the key ingredients in performance and compensation reviews. Though there were other dimensions, these measures were known to be the most important. Thus, despite the exhortations of top management to respond to the market, middle managers knew what the reality was. They agreed that market considerations were important (as shown on the commitment map). The real priorities, however, were based on what senior management rewarded.

From Understanding to Influence: Acquiring the Skills

In the analysis of our research data, we consistently find an association between strategic understanding and strategic involvement, but which comes first? The answer is, both. Involvement and understanding have a reciprocal, reinforcing relationship. Thus, understanding—building your own and the organization's strategic knowledge base—is an important prerequisite to assuming any one of the four roles. Ultimately, however, to grow in strategic awareness and to have influence middle managers have to *get involved*.

Resource B is a self-test of the extent to which a middle manager performs the strategic roles. Be honest. After taking the test, compare your scores with those in our research sample (reported at the outset of this chapter and summarized in Figure 10.1). Later, after you have an opportunity to improve your strategic understanding and influencing skills, take the self-test again to see whether your level of involvement has increased.

If you are like most middle managers, you will find that you score higher on implementation and lower on the roles that emphasize upward influence and divergent thinking. If innovation is the key strategy priority within your firm, however, you may need to rethink the importance of championing and facilitating in your work. Taking the first steps toward effective strategic influence is not as hard as it may seem.

The way to get started is to *have deliberate conversations.* Whether with peers, subordinates, or superiors, begin to talk about the company strategy. There are some organizational climates in which discussion of basic goals and directions seems off-limits, but usually this is not intentional. Avoid global comments at first, and focus interactions on specific issues, such as technical refinements or changes in customer needs. Focusing on smaller issues allows you to get involved and learn more about strategy without appearing to challenge it. Build and use the intraorganizational network to form a sense of what people are thinking and what their priorities are. Look for both divergence and integration among the multitude of inputs you seek. This process almost always creates an opportunity to bring something useful to the attention of top management. Maybe it is a customer service problem, a technical glitch or a new product opportunity. Remember, synthesizing information is a precursor to championing.

But many mangers avoid the risk of these interactions. Communicating effectively in any context—but especially in a face-to-face interaction with senior management—requires confidence, eloquence, and some degree of polish. Knowledge of the strategy gives you the vocabulary of influence, but there are other, equally important management skills that are essential to successful strategic involvement.

Leading from the Middle: The Core Skills of Strategic Influence

Middle managers face a complex leadership situation. Not only are they expected to lead subordinates, but unlike the upper and lower echelons, they must also lead in an upward direction. Middle managers are positioned in the middle of the strategic decision process and this presents both challenges and opportunities. Top managers are trying to drive their priorities down, while operating levels send a sometimes conflicting stream of priorities upward. This upward, emergent flow is created by the ongoing need to develop responses to unforeseen events. Middle managers are expected to carry out top management's intent, react to daily crises, and plan for the future of the business. Only a skillful leader is likely to survive. Figure 10.3 summarizes the four areas of skill development needed for each of the four roles.

Figure 10.3. Relative Importance of Managerial Skills in the Strategic Roles.

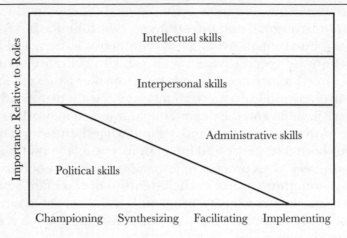

Political Skills

Political ability means understanding how your words or behavior affect the perceived self-interests of other individuals and groups in the organization. It is important in all four strategic roles, but political skills are likely to become the limiting factor earliest in the championing role. It is here that the middle manager is called on to take risks, to think like an entrepreneur, and to go beyond the predetermined plan.

In the formal proposal stages of championing, for example, managers often make presentations in front of virtual strangers. In many cases, they may not even know who is reviewing the written documentation. The relationships encountered are intermittent both in terms of frequency of contact and variety of people involved. Having an influence within such a "nominal" group requires keen sensitivity to the political forces in the organization. Inevitably, proposals for change create winners and losers. If a new business venture is being championed, for example, someone will see it as a grab for resources. If a process improvement is the goal, there may be personnel implications.

The champion, therefore, should create an inventory of expected opponents and supporters. Before bringing the proposal to the attention of top management, each individual or group represented on the list should be given attention. Communication should be informal, and the proposal should be presented at this stage as though it were tentative, subject to revision based on the needs of the party in question. Rosabeth Kanter describes a process she calls "tin cupping," where middle managers negotiate informal support in exchange for future or past reciprocities.[7] The concerns of opponents should be incorporated, and when this is not possible, they should at least be acknowledged as valid issues to be dealt with in the implementation stage.

The synthesizing role follows closely in terms of its political challenge. Championing cannot be successful without an earlier effort to set the agenda, establish a context, or define the threat/ opportunity. The use of tact in strategic conversations can be crucial to learning from others and maintaining a nondefensive posture in communicating what you know. The classic mistake is to appear overly critical of one's superiors. Early in your experience, top management's deliberate strategy may seem wrongheaded or shortsighted. Keep an open mind, however. Often, the more you learn the better top management looks, and premature criticism can cut off the learning and communicating process altogether.

Though it is oriented more toward subordinates, facilitating requires an understanding of "what you can get away with" in terms of slack resources and openness within the unit. Needless to say, you will not be discovering these limits in the company's formal procedures. Instead, facilitating relies on finding individuals who will share information about tolerances with the control system and about the idiosyncrasies of individual contributors. Identifying such confidants frequently requires an assessment of who around you has the most to gain or lose from a close relationship.

Finally, implementing deliberate strategy means "being a good soldier" and does not require going outside the official strategy. Nevertheless, the politics involved can frequently be a source of frustration even to the most talented administrator. Thousands of middle managers have discovered, for example, that implementing a downsizing strategy causes enormous physical and emotional stress, no matter how much they understand and agree with the rationale.[8]

While political sensitivity is vital to effective strategic influence, nothing will limit a manager's potential for influence quicker than being seen by others as a *self*-interested politician. The political nature of organizations must be recognized and managed, but middle managers should approach this with the *organization's* interest in mind. In addition to knowing what those interests are (in other words, understanding the strategy), this requires humility and moral backbone. In the end, no amount of strategic understanding or political skill can compensate for a lack of character.

Administrative Skills: Negotiating the Formal Organization

We define administrative skill as the ability to operate successfully within the formal organization context and to create new aspects of formal organization (procedures, job descriptions, performance plans, and so on) whenever necessary. Formal organization creates a degree of certainty and stability within which a group of individuals can collaborate and coordinate their activity. Every organization has a set of bureaucratic realities. These are frequently taken for granted, but our advice is to study carefully how the game is played. There may be opportunities to champion change in the bureaucracy, but you cannot tackle such a task without understanding the critical variables in the system.

Lack of skill in this arena can undermine effectiveness in any of the roles. Otherwise successful proposals have been shot down because of middle manager ignorance or disdain for following procedure and gaining appropriate sign-offs. Similarly, an awareness of formal information channels can be critical in the synthesizing process. Unless one appreciates the formal hierarchy, for example, interpreting and communicating information within the organization can be political suicide.

In the end, however, administrative skills are most prominent in the implementing and facilitating roles since these require resource commitments. Implementing involves creating formal arrangements—new structures and new policies or procedures—that align with a change in strategy. Making the translation from intent to tangible action relies heavily on detailed definition of new roles and processes. Typically, controls and incentives also require adjustment. Successful facilitating, on the other hand, requires a good understanding of the existing administrative context, how control systems work, and how discretion can be achieved. Nurturing informality and experimentation can only be accomplished if the administrative "umbrella" is adjusted to allow people room to maneuver informally while avoiding official sanction.

Intellectual and Interpersonal Skills

It will come as no surprise that intelligence and interpersonal competence are required of strategic middle managers. Nonetheless it is worth emphasizing that stepping into strategy requires a quantum leap in the levels of both these skill sets. Operations is much more definite and stable than strategy—both in terms of what one needs to know and who one interacts with. Becoming a strategic player therefore means coping with a great deal of uncertainty and equivocality. In addition, the roles themselves typically are not defined formally within the organization. Strategic middle managers are left to find their own way, rather than being directed by those above them.

The intellectual challenge in working within such ambiguity is to create a mental framework of the organization's circumstance and its pattern of strategic responses. This means building a mental model and testing it in the real world. Revision depends on how well the theory performs as a framework for guiding managerial action.

Although many managers may be uncomfortable with this idea, everyone operates within a mental framework, whether it is explicit or not. The successful strategist, however, is deliberate about the learning process; as a result she is effectively working with less ambiguity than those who are less intentional. In a very real sense, she understands more about what is going on around her and is in a better position to act.

On the interpersonal side, the key point to remember is that strategy is not so much the result of a decision as it is the outcome of a social learning process. Managers who understand this may develop an appreciation for the importance of the "touchy-feely" side of their job. Without skills in communicating (sending and receiving), trust building (sharing information and encouraging openness in others), and leading (directing others and sharing power), middle managers are in no position to take on any of the roles in strategy, no matter how good their ideas may be.

Most readers will nod their heads on hearing of the importance of interpersonal and leadership skills to management, but only a minority will achieve the level of proficiency needed to be a force in strategy. The skills of interpersonal competence require first and foremost a high level of self-awareness, and we have found this to be the single greatest barrier to self-improvement. Unless one is willing to admit that the development of people skills requires continuous self-improvement, the adjustment to the new and unforeseen interactions in the strategic roles will be difficult, if not impossible.

Internal and External Sources for Acquiring the Skills of a Strategist

We have found that political and administrative skills tend to be honed best on the job, whereas interpersonal and intellectual skills lend themselves to development in settings outside the organization. The list below identifies some of the ways managers can begin the developmental process.

Development Sources for Managerial Skill Sets

- Internal sources of political and administrative skill development

  Mentorship
  Job rotation
  Cross-functional teams

- External sources of interpersonal and intellectual skill development

  M.B.A. programs
  Professional seminars
  Consultants

Of all the internal sources, a successful mentor relationship is easily the most important—and probably the rarest. The number of mentors in senior positions who have the requisite knowledge base to help managers facing today's realities is quite small. In addition, the task of mentoring usually offers few formal rewards, and mentors risk the possibility that their time will be invested without so much as a "thank you" from the beneficiary. Indeed, the aspiring middle manager looking for a mentor is often his own worst enemy.

We recommend that young managers look for signs of unselfishness among the senior executive group as the first step to finding a mentor. Giving credit to others and spending time on the success of others are clear markers of the potential mentor. Once someone has been identified, the potential apprentice must avoid assuming that a relationship will develop. As in all relationships, a courting period is required, filled with lunches, recreation, and other opportunities for informal discussion. Mentoring does not always evolve out of friendship, but good feelings are important to making the process work.

Externally, M.B.A. programs have become the subject of much derision in the business press, and in fact, many programs deserve the criticism. Business schools too are renewing themselves and restructuring, however. In particular, many of the better programs now offer more intellectual content of use to the potential strategic middle manager. Look for national accreditation, and talk to professors and students before enrolling. We believe an M.B.A. from a recently revamped program is an excellent place to start.

One of the fundamental problems, however, is that the M.B.A. program tends to be "one size fits all." You may find that you can benefit more from specialized courses that are tailored directly to your personal shortcomings. This is particularly true for the leadership and interpersonal components, because the classroom environment of the M.B.A. still tends to be weakest in these areas.

Remember, managing is a *process,* not a *position.* It is too easy to become fixated on defending the status quo. Changes in the position of middle managers are inevitable. Ignoring the challenge of the strategic roles presented here will result in the realization of the manager's worst fear. Those who focus on the process, however—who throw themselves into the flow of realized strategy—will encounter exciting opportunities for personal and professional reward.

Conclusion

Large, complex business organizations are here to stay. Their importance to the economic vitality of our society is increasing and will continue to do so. Society is increasingly dependent on these institutions to deliver products and services that improve the quality of our lives and to provide a stable source of employment.

As our society evolves, however, the challenges and pressures facing large business firms are also changed and altered. Accordingly, over the last generation the profession of management has been fundamentally transformed. The pendulum has swung from merely managing stability to continuously searching for improvement and innovation. Although the transition has often been difficult, in the end the rewards are great: not only in terms of the renewed competitiveness of U.S. industry but also in the quality of managerial work. At no time in our history have the opportunities in large business organizations been greater. We hope our readers have come to recognize the exciting possibilities and challenges facing today's manager, have gained some insight into how to pursue these, and as important, have become convinced of their potential to make a strategic difference.

Resource A:
The Strategic Consensus Questionnaire[1]

Instructions: These items assess the relative importance of reducing costs and increasing differentiation in an organization's competition strategy.[2] Managers participating in the survey should circle the number that represents the relative importance of each item in describing their organization's strategic priorities.

1. Reducing the overall costs of operations

Very unimportant	Neutral	Very important
1————2————3————4————5		

2. Stressing new products and services

Very unimportant	Neutral	Very important
1————2————3————4————5		

3. Focusing primarily on high-margin customer groups

Very unimportant	Neutral	Very important
1————2————3————4————5		

---

1.   Permission is granted to reproduce this questionnaire for internal nonprofit company use. If this questionnaire is to be used in a compilation for profit, please contact Jossey-Bass for permission.

2.   The items in this questionnaire are based on the theory of generic strategies in Michael Porter's book *Competitive Strategy* (New York: Free Press, 1980). When assessing the strategy of any particular company, it is useful to tailor the questionnaire to the language and concerns of the specific context. As an initial measure of management consensus, however, we have found that this standardized approach works well.

4. Offering highly differentiated (unique) products or services

Very unimportant		Neutral		Very important
1	2	3	4	5

5. Spending more on advertising than competitors

Very unimportant		Neutral		Very important
1	2	3	4	5

6. Offering a broad line of products or services

Very unimportant		Neutral		Very important
1	2	3	4	5

7. Pricing products and services competitively

Very unimportant		Neutral		Very important
1	2	3	4	5

8. Offering specialized products and services

Very unimportant		Neutral		Very important
1	2	3	4	5

9. Maintaining a trim organization and lean staff levels

Very unimportant		Neutral		Very important
1	2	3	4	5

10. Increasing the level of automation in operations

Very unimportant		Neutral		Very important
1	2	3	4	5

11. Selling large volumes of standard products or services

Very unimportant		Neutral		Very important
1	2	3	4	5

12. Gaining a large market share

Very unimportant		Neutral		Very important
1	2	3	4	5

13. Maintaining a high level of employee motivation and satisfaction

Very
unimportant   Neutral   Very
important
1————2————3————4————5

14. Compensating employees at above average levels

Very
unimportant   Neutral   Very
important
1————2————3————4————5

15. Providing incentives for employees to reduce costs

Very
unimportant   Neutral   Very
important
1————2————3———— 4————5

16. Segmenting the market to identify profitable customer groups

Very
unimportant   Neutral   Very
important
1————2————3———— 4————5

17. Emphasizing operational efficiencies

Very
unimportant   Neutral   Very
important
1————2————3———— 4————5

18. Building name recognition and corporate image

Very
unimportant   Neutral   Very
important
1————2————3———— 4————5

19. Focusing on special market needs

Very
unimportant   Neutral   Very
important
1————2————3———— 4————5

Scoring Key

Emphasis on cost   Add scores on items
as a strategic priority: 1, 7, 9, 10, 11, 12, 15, 17
                           Divide the sum by 8
                           Multiply the result by 2

Emphasis on differentiation as a strategic priority:	Add scores on items 2, 3, 4, 5, 6, 8, 13, 14, 16, 18, 19 Divide the sum by 11 Multiply the result by 2

The scoring results will produce numbers from 1 to 10 representing the relative importance of cost and differentiation (1 = low, 10 = high). Each individual's score can then be represented on a grid with these scales on each axis, as in Figure 10.2.

Resource B: A Self-Test of Middle Management Strategic Involvement

Instructions: In your experience as a manager, how frequently have you performed the following activities? Circle a number for each item.

1. Monitor and assess the impact of changes in the organization's external environment.
Never	Rarely	Occasionally	Regularly	Frequently
1	2	3	4	5

2. Implement action plans designed to meet top management objectives.
Never	Rarely	Occasionally	Regularly	Frequently
1	2	3	4	5

3. Integrate information from a variety of sources to communicate its strategic significance.
Never	Rarely	Occasionally	Regularly	Frequently
1	2	3	4	5

4. Evaluate the merits of new proposals.
Never	Rarely	Occasionally	Regularly	Frequently
1	2	3	4	5

5. Evaluate the merits of proposals generated in my unit, encouraging some, discouraging others.
Never	Rarely	Occasionally	Regularly	Frequently
1	2	3	4	5

6. Translate organizational goals into objectives for individuals
Never	Rarely	Occasionally	Regularly	Frequently
1	2	3	4	5

7. Provide a safe haven for experimental programs.

Never   Rarely   Occasionally   Regularly   Frequently
1—————2—————3—————4—————5

8. Assess and communicate the business-level implications of new information to higher-level managers.

Never   Rarely   Occasionally   Regularly   Frequently
1—————2—————3—————4—————5

9. Search for new opportunities and bring them to the attention of higher-level managers.

Never   Rarely   Occasionally   Regularly   Frequently
1—————2—————3—————4—————5

10. Communicate and sell top management initiatives to subordinates.

Never   Rarely   Occasionally   Regularly   Frequently
1—————2—————3—————4—————5

11. Define and justify the role of new programs or processes to upper-level managers.

Never   Rarely   Occasionally   Regularly   Frequently
1—————2—————3—————4—————5

12. Encourage multidisciplinary problem-solving teams.

Never   Rarely   Occasionally   Regularly   Frequently
1—————2—————3—————4—————5

13. Proactively seek information about your business from customers, suppliers, competitors, business publications, and so on.

Never   Rarely   Occasionally   Regularly   Frequently
1—————2—————3—————4—————5

14. Monitor and communicate to higher-level managers the activities of competitors, suppliers, and other outside organizations.

Never   Rarely   Occasionally   Regularly   Frequently
1—————2—————3—————4—————5

15. Justify to higher-level managers programs that have already been established.

Never   Rarely   Occasionally   Regularly   Frequently
1—————2—————3—————4—————5

16. Provide resources and develop objectives/strategies for unofficial projects.

Never	Rarely	Occasionally	Regularly	Frequently
1———————2———————3———————4———————5				

17. Translate organizational goals into departmental action plans.

Never	Rarely	Occasionally	Regularly	Frequently
1———————2———————3———————4———————5				

18. Relax regulations and procedures in order to get new projects started.

Never	Rarely	Occasionally	Regularly	Frequently
1———————2———————3———————4———————5				

19. Propose new programs or projects to higher-level managers.

Never	Rarely	Occasionally	Regularly	Frequently
1———————2———————3———————4———————5				

20. Monitor activities within your unit to ensure that they support top management objectives.

Never	Rarely	Occasionally	Regularly	Frequently
1———————2———————3———————4———————5				

Scoring Key

Championing: Add your scores on items 4, 9, 11, 15, and 19.   *17*
Facilitating: Add your scores on items 5, 7, 12, 16, and 18.   *18*
Synthesizing: Add your scores on items 1, 3, 8, 13, and 14.   *17*
Implementing: Add your scores on items 2, 6, 10, 17, and 20.   *18*

Less than 10:	You almost never perform this role.
10 to 15:	You rarely or occasionally perform this role.
16 to 20:	You regularly or at least occasionally perform this role.
Over 20:	You regularly or frequently perform this role.

Notes

Preface

1. Bernard Wysocki, Jr., "Some Companies Cut Costs Too Far, Suffer Corporate Anorexia," *Wall Street Journal,* July 5, 1995, p. 1.

2. Richard A. D'Aveni, *Hypercompetition: Managing the Dynamics of Strategic Maneuvering* (New York: Free Press, 1994).

Chapter One

1. "65 Years of Work in America," *Business Week,* October 17, 1994, p. 109.

Chapter Two

1. See Gary Hamel and C. K. Prahalad, "Strategic Intent," *Harvard Business Review,* May-June 1989, pp. 63–76, for a more detailed discussion.

2. R. Hall, "The Strategic Analysis of Intangible Resources," *Strategic Management Journal,* 1992, *13,* 135–144.

3. For a study of information flows and middle management, see M. D. Hutt, P. H. Reingen, and J. R. Ronchetto, "Tracing Emergent Processes in Marketing Strategy Formation," *Journal of Marketing,* 1988, *52,* 4–19.

4. *Making Strategy Work: The Challenge of the 1990s* is a report available from Booz-Allen Hamilton Inc., 101 Park Avenue, New York, NY 10178.

5. This description of VTR development borrows heavily from an article by Richard S. Rosenbloom and Michael A. Cusumano, "Technological Pioneering and Competitive Advantage: The Birth of the VCR Industry," *California Management Review,* 1987, *29,* reprinted in Michael L. Tushman and William L. Moore (eds.), *Readings in the Management of Innovation,* 2nd ed. (New York: HarperBusiness, 1982), 3–22.

6. W. D. Guth and Ian C. MacMillan, "Strategy Implementation Versus Middle Management Self-Interest," *Strategic Management Journal*, 1986, *7*, 313–327.

7. Dorothy Leonard-Barton, "Core Capabilities and Core Rigidities: A Paradox in Managing New Product Development," *Strategic Management Journal*, 1992, *13*, 111–125.

Chapter Three

1. W. Cascio, "Downsizing: What Do We Know? What Have We Learned?" *Academy of Management Executive*, 1993, *7*, 95–104.

2. B. J. Wysocki, "Some Companies Cut Costs Too Far, Suffer Corporate Anorexia," *The Wall Street Journal*, July 5, 1995, p. 1.

3. Daniel Burrus, *Technotrends: How You Can Go Beyond Your Competition by Applying Tomorrow's Technology Today* (New York: HarperCollins, 1994).

4. Wayne Cascio, "Downsizing: What Do We Know? What Have We Learned?" *Academy of Management Executive*, 1993, *7*, 95–104.

5. Cascio, "Downsizing," p. 97–98.

6. Mohamed E. Hussein, "The Dynamic Repositioning of Analysis and Technology, Inc.," University of Connecticut working paper (1994).

7. Cascio, "Downsizing," p. 100.

8. "Redefining the Middle Manager," *HR Executive Review*, 1995, *II*(2), 3–18.

9. See, for example, D. A. Heenan, "The Downside of Downsizing," *Journal of Business Strategy*, Nov.-Dec. 1989, pp. 18–23.

Chapter Four

1. See, for example, Henry Mintzberg, "The Design School: Reconsidering the Basic Premises of Strategic Management," *Strategic Management Journal*, Mar.-Apr. 1990, 171–195.

2. This example is based on the account reported by Richard Pascale in "Perspectives on Strategy: The Real Story Behind Honda's Success," *California Management Review*, 1984, *26*(3), 47–72.

3. H. Mintzberg, and J. Waters, "Of Strategies Deliberate and Emergent," *Strategic Management Journal*, 1985, *6*, 257–272.

4. James Brian Quinn, *Strategies for Change: Logical Incrementalism*, (Burr Ridge, Ill.: Irwin, 1980).

5. B. Wooldridge, and S. W. Floyd, "The Strategy Process, Middle Management Involvement, and Organizational Performance," *Strategic Management Journal*, 1990, *11*(3), 231–241.

6. Although our five steps roughly parallel those found in conventional descriptions of the strategic process (in other words, goal

formation, alternative generation, evaluation, choice, and implementation), in order to reduce the risk of biasing results we avoided words such as *formulation* and *implementation*.

7. Wooldridge and Floyd (see note five).

8. Joseph L. Bower, *Managing the Resource Allocation Process* (Boston: Harvard Business School, 1970).

9. J. D. Thompson, *Organizations in Action* (New York: McGraw-Hill, 1967).

10. R. H. Kanter, *The Change Masters* (New York: Basic Books, 1983).

11. Kanter (see note ten).

12. Some of these findings were published in our article "Middle Management Involvement in Strategy and Its Association with Strategic Type," *Strategic Management Journal*, 1992, *13*, 153–167.

13. Stuart Hart and Catherine Banbury, "How Strategy-Making Processes Can Make a Difference," *Strategic Management Journal*, 1994, *15*, 251–269.

14. Regression analysis was used to examine the relationship between managerial behavior and organizational performance. This analysis indicated that organizations whose middle managers reported varying levels of upward influence behavior tended to perform better ($R^2 = .19$, $p < .001$).

15. See our article "Dinosaurs or Dynamos? Recognizing Middle Management's Strategic Role," *Academy of Management Executive*, 1994, *8*, 47–57.

16. With apologies to Henry Mintzberg, who defined strategy as a "stream of decisions," we think the pace and scope of activities in today's organizations justify a slightly grander metaphor.

Chapter Five

1. Tracy Kidder, "Flying Upside Down," *Atlantic Monthly*, July 1981, pp. 54–64. Copyright © 1981, Tracy Kidder. Ironically, the publication of Kidder's story just preceded a period during which middle management's value would begin to be discounted. Although we found many other examples in our own data and report them elsewhere in the book, we draw from this experience to highlight the champion's attributes. The indented material that follows is quoted or adapted from this article.

2. H. Edward Wrapp, "Good Managers Don't Make Policy Decisions," *Harvard Business Review*, Sept.-Oct. 1967.

3. See Jane E. Dutton and Susan J. Ashford, "Selling Issues to Top Management," *Academy of Management Review*, 1993, *18*, 397–428.

4. For a discussion of how inertia and stress builds within a strategic course, see J. O. Huff, A. S. Huff, and H. Thomas, "Strategic Renewal

and the Interaction of Cumulative Stress and Inertia," *Strategic Management Journal,* 1992, *13,* 55–75.

5. Tom Brown, "Gray-Cloud Manager," *Industry Week,* Oct. 5, 1992, p. 71.

6. Brown, "Gray-Cloud Manager," p. 71.

Chapter Six

1. Richard Pascale, "Perspectives on Strategy: The Real Story Behind Honda's Success," *California Management Review,* 1984, *26*(3), 47–72.

2. Michael Porter, "Toward a Dynamic Model of Strategy," *Strategic Management Journal,* Special issue, Winter 1991, *12,* 95–118.

3. We use the word *potential* here because we have found that middle managers are not always as outgoing as they could be. I. Nonaka describes the crucial role of middle managers in the organization's information network in his article "Toward Middle-Up-Down Management: Accelerating Information Creation," *Sloan Management Review,* Spring 1988, pp. 9–18. Michael D. Hutt, Peter H. Reingen, and John R. Ronchetto, Jr., reached a similar conclusion in "Tracing Emergent Processes in Marketing Strategy Formation," *Journal of Marketing,* January 1988, *52,* pp. 4–19.

4. For the theory underlying the notion of how categories influence shared organizational understandings, see Jane E. Dutton and Susan E. Jackson, "Categorizing Strategic Issues: Links to Organization Action," *Academy of Management Review,* 1987, *12,* 76–90.

5. This discussion is taken from Jane E. Dutton and Susan J. Ashford, "Selling Issues to Top Management," *Academy of Management Review,* 1993, *18,* 397–428.

6. Dutton and Ashford (see note five).

7. Readers interested in the research basis for this argument could begin by reading Irving Janis, *Victims of Groupthink* (Boston: Houghton-Mifflin, 1972) and David M. Schweiger, W. R. Sandberg, and J. W. Ragan, "Group Approaches for Improving Strategic Decision Making: A Comparative Analysis of Dialectical Inquiry, Devil's Advocacy, and Consensus," *Academy of Management Journal,* 1986, *29,* 51–71.

8. Janis (see note seven).

Chapter Seven

1. For an excellent discussion of this cycle, see J. O. Huff, A. S. Huff, and H. Thomas, "Strategic Renewal and the Interaction of Cumulative Stress and Inertia," *Strategic Management Journal,* 1992, *13,* 55–75.

2. Readers interested in the theoretical and research foundations behind this pattern of social change may be interested in a recent discussion by C. G. Gersisk in "Revolutionary Change Theories: A Multilevel Exploration of the Punctuated Equilibrium Paradigm," *Academy of Management Review,* 1991, *16,* 10–36. Michael Tushman and Elaine Romanelli are often credited with early formulations of the idea in "Organizational Evolution: A Metamorphosis Model of Convergence and Reorientation," in L. L. Cummings and B. M. Staw (eds.), *Research in Organizational Behavior,* 7, 171–222, (Greenwich, Conn.: JAI Press).

3. Michael Tushman and David Nadler, who have written volumes on the ways managers should organize for innovation, consistently make this point. For a good summary of their ideas on this issue, see M. Tushman and D. Nadler, "Organizing for Innovation," *California Management Review,* 1986, *28*(3), 74–92.

4. John Kotter and James Heskett found in their study that crisis and new leadership at the top were the two main ingredients preceding major corporate change. See their book *Corporate Culture and Organizational Performance* (New York: Free Press, 1992).

5. A study of the relationship between good citizenship and elements of job satisfaction, such as promotions and pay, can be found in T. M. Bateman and D. M. Organ, "Job Satisfaction and the Good Soldier: The Relationship Between Affect and Employee 'Citizenship,'" *Academy of Management Journal,* 1983, *26*(4), 587–595.

6. Joseph Schumpeter, *Capitalism, Socialism, and Democracy* (3rd ed.) (New York: HarperCollins, 1950).

7. Joseph L. Bower, *Managing the Resource Allocation Process* (Boston: Harvard Business School, 1970, pp. 219–239).

8. We interviewed top managers in twenty-one companies as part of our study reported in "The Strategy Process, Middle Management Involvement, and Organizational Performance," *Strategic Management Journal,* 1990, *11,* 231–241.

9. We define managers' understanding and commitment toward strategy as *strategic consensus.* Interested readers should see our article "Strategic Consensus: The Key to Effective Implementation," *Academy of Management Executive,* 1992, *6,* 27–39.

10. The historical relationship between the top and middle levels in many companies has produced an atmosphere of mistrust. Middle managers become suspicious and defensive about practically any top management initiative.

11. On the "importation" of ideas from outside, see P. S. Ring and A. H. Van De Ven, "Formal and Informal Dimensions of Transac-

tions," in A. H. Van De Ven, H. L. Angle, and M. S. Poole (eds.), *Research on the Management of Innovation* (New York: HarperCollins, 1989, pp. 171–192). Robert Burgelman used ecological theory in his description of innovation at Intel in his article "Intraorganizational Ecology of Strategy Making and Organizational Adaptation: Theory and Field Research," *Organizational Science*, 1991, *2*, 239–262.

12. W. Dyer, *Team Building: Issues and Alternatives* (Reading, Mass.: Addison-Wesley, 1977).

13. Chris Argyris is one of the earliest and most consistent voices on the link between trust, openness, and organizational information sharing, beginning with his book *Integrating the Individual and the Organization* (New York: Wiley, 1964).

Chapter Eight

1. Robert A. Burgelman was the first to make the distinction between autonomous and induced strategic behavior in his article "A Model of the Interaction of Strategic Behavior, Corporate Context, and the Concept of Strategy," *Academy of Management Review*, 1983, *8*, 61–70.

2. Gary Hamel and C. K. Prahalad coined the expression *strategic intent,* and it has been widely adopted as a term that expresses the kind of strategic direction top managers should articulate. (See their article by that name in the *Harvard Business Review*, May-June 1989, pp. 63–76.

3. *Making Strategy Work: The Challenge of the 1990s* is a 1990 report available from Booz-Allen Hamilton Inc., 101 Park Avenue, New York, NY 10178.

4. See, for example, L. Dobyns and C. Crawford-Mason, *Quality or Else: The Revolution in World Business* (Boston: Houghton-Mifflin, 1991); and L. Munroe-Faure and M. Munroe-Faure, *Implementing Total Quality Management* (London: Pitman, 1992).

5. C. M. Fiol and A. S. Huff have described the concept of organization identity in their article "Maps for Managers: Where Are We? Where Do We Go from Here?" *Journal of Management*, 1992, *17*, 191–211.

6. Psychologists have identified discrepancy theory as one of the most important ways to think about how people change behavior. See N. Cantor and J. F. Kihlstrom, *Personality and Social Intelligence* (Englewood Cliffs, N.J.: Prentice-Hall, 1987).

7. The discussion of TQM implementation strategy is based on an article by R. K. Reger, L. T. Gustafson, S. M. Demarie, and J. V. Mul-

lane, "Reframing the Organization: Why Implementing Total Quality Is Easier Said Than Done," *Academy of Management Review*, 1994, *19*, 565–584.

8. M. C. Tushman, W. H. Newman, and E. Romanelli, "Managing the Unsteady Pace of Organizational Evolution," *California Management Review*, 1986, *24*(1), 29–44.

9. See, for example, P. C. Nutt, "Identifying and Appraising How Managers Install Strategy," *Strategic Management Journal*, Jan.-Feb. 1987, pp. 1–14; D. K. Hurst, "Of Boxes, Bubbles, and Effective Management," *Harvard Business Review*, May-June 1984, pp. 78–88.

Chapter Nine

1. Peter Drucker was among the first to make such a prediction in "The New Organization," *Harvard Business Review*, Jan.-Feb. 1988. More recently, such prognoses have increased as firms have continued to reduce the numbers of their middle managers; see, for example, "Face to Face: The Future of Middle Managers," *Management Review*, Sept. 1993.

2. Elliott Jaques, "In Praise of Hierarchy," *Harvard Business Review*, Jan.-Feb. 1990, p. 127.

3. Michael Lubatkin and Dean Ulizio, "Motorola," in Arthur Thompson and A. J. Strickland (eds.), *Strategic Management: Concept and Cases*. (Homewood, Ill.: Irwin, 1996).

4. Texas Instruments' organization is depicted on page 119 of Hammer and Champy's book *Reengineering the Corporation* (New York: HarperBusiness).

5. Alain Pinsonneault and Kenneth L. Kraemer, "The Impact of Information Technology on Middle Managers," *Management Information Systems Quarterly*, Sept. 1993, pp. 271–292.

6. Pinsonneault and Kraemer, "The Impact of Information Technology," p. 284.

7. John N. Sheridan, "Turning Foremen into CEOs," *Industry Week*, Feb. 6, 1989, pp. 21–24.

8. Readers interested in the puny payoffs from IT investments should see T. N. Warner's article "Information Technology as a Competitive Burden," *Sloan Management Review*, 1987, *29*(1), 55–61. D. Boddy and D. Buchanan examine similar effects in white-collar contexts in their article "Information Technology and Productivity: Myths and Realities," *OMEGA*, 1984, *12*(3), 233–340.

9. Paul Strassman's book *Information Payoff* (New York: Free Press, 1985) describes many of the problems this creates.

10. *Making Strategy Work: The Challenge of the 1990s* is a report available from Booz-Allen Hamilton Inc., 101 Park Avenue, New York, NY 10178.

11. Reported in *Fortune*, Dec. 4, 1989, p. 58.

12. Kenneth Labick, "Making Over Middle Managers," *Fortune*, May 8, 1989, pp. 58–64.

13. David B. Balkin summarized this approach in the article "Managing Employee Separations with the Reward System," *Academy of Management Executive*, 1992, *6*(4), 64–69.

14. Reasons for the disconnection between organizational capability and advantage are both theoretical and practical. R. Reed and R. DeFillipi discuss the theoretical issues in "Causal Ambiguity, Barriers to Imitation and Sustainable Competitive Advantage," *Academy of Management Review*, 1990, *15*, 88–102.

15. Thomas A. Stewart, "How to Lead a Revolution," *Fortune*, November 28, 1994, p. 54.

Chapter Ten

1. D. M. Reid, "Operationalizing Strategic Planning," *Strategic Management Journal*, 1989, *10*, 553–567.

2. Francis Westley uses the conversational metaphor to great advantage in his article "Middle Managers and Strategy: Microdynamics of Inclusion," *Strategic Management Journal*, 1990, *11*, 337–351.

3. These quotations are from middle managers in a survey about changing jobs, *Industry Week*, Jan. 2, 1989, pp. 11–12.

4. Our description of this process is written from a middle management perspective, but senior managers may also find the exercise interesting. For a detailed description of the procedure we use to map strategic consensus, see our article "Managing Strategic Consensus: The Foundation of Effective Implementation," *Academy of Management Executive*, 1992, *6*(4), 27–39.

5. In consulting practice, we custom tailor the questionnaire so that it is phrased in the words that are commonly used within the organization. This provides a much richer picture of the patterns of consensus.

6. It is ironic that although most people have never even thought about their organization's strategy, when you ask them whether they know the strategy, they immediately feel guilty for their "ignorance."

7. See Rosabeth Kanter, *The Change Masters* (New York: Basic Books, 1983).

8. David Noer has written eloquently about middle management and survivor's syndrome in *Healing the Wounds: Overcoming the Trauma of Layoffs and Revitalizing Downsized Organizations,* San Francisco: Jossey-Bass, 1993. Also see Lee Smith, "Burned-Out Bosses," *Fortune,* July 25, 1994, pp. 44–52, for some dramatic testimonials.

Index